MYCENAE-EPIDAURUS
TIRYNS - NAUPLION

Complete guide to the archaeological sites of Argolis with
full-colour illustrations, maps, plans and reconstructions

CLIO EDITIONS
athens 1978

Translation by: HELEN BACOYIANIS - PETRONOTIS

Art layout: RACHEL MISDRACHE - CAPON

Phototype-setting: FOTRON S.A.

Photographs: S. TSAVDAROGLOU, M. SKIADARESSES,
N. KONTOS

Copyright 1978 "CLIO" Editions

No part of this publication (text, photographs and plans) may be
reproduced in any form or by any means without the publisher's prior
consent.

NICOS PAPAHATZIS: Archaeologist

MYCENAE - EPIDAURUS
TIRYNS - NAUPLION

HERAION OF ARGOS-ARGOS-ASINE-LERNA-TROEZEN

CONTENTS

CHRONOLOGICAL DATA

I. MYTHICAL AND HISTORICAL ARGOLIS
1. Its wealth of traditions
2. The mythical past of Argolis in relation to data from excavations
3. Historical period

II. TOPOGRAPHICAL SURVEY OF ANCIENT ARGOLIS
1. Boundaries of ancient Argolis. Bordering Corinthian sites
2. Ancient and contemporary road-approaches from Corinth
3. Ancient sites southwest of Argos
4. Ancient sites northwest of Argos
5. Ancient sites to the east of Argos
6. The road to Nauplion - Epidaurus. Ancient Epidauria
7. Troezen
8. Hermionis
9. Asine
10. Nauplia
11. Lerna
12. Thyreatis

III. EXCAVATIONS IN ARGOLIS
1. The history of excavations
2. Mycenae
3. The Heraeum of Argos
4. Argos
5. Tiryns
6. The Asclepieion of Epidaurus

CHRONOLOGICAL DATA

The outstanding periods in the history of Argolis (especially those concerning its prehistoric past)

A. Before the Bronze Age

The oldest settlements, which have been identified with certainty, in Argolis belong to the M e s o l i t h i c a g e, at a time when the cultivation of cereals was still unknown and men lived by hunting, fishing, or the gathering of the available fruit and nuts.

A settlement of the 8th millennium B.C. has been identified with certainty opposite the contemporary village of Koilada in Hermionis, at a location near homeric Mases, that is, in a deep cave at P h r a g h t h i. This settlement was still in existence during the late neolithic period.

A settlement of an older era than the Neolithic, (probably one of the end of the Mesolithic age) was located six kilometres south of Argos, at the exact site of the Erasinos springs, in the caves of K e p h a l a r i. Due to the abundance of water, this settlement survived through the neolithic era, up to the Bronze age.

Another settlement of the early Neolithic age, (of the beginning of the 5th millennium B.C.), has been identified on a low hill at L e r n a, near the springs of water that flow past that site, a short distance from the sea. This settlement, as well, was in existence at the end of the Neolithic age (up until the beginning of the 3rd millennium B.C.).

Beginning with the mature neolithic age (from the 4th millennium to the beginning of the 3rd millennium B.C.), remains of settlements are to be found in a considerable number of sites, Tiryns and Prosymna (the Heraeum of Argos) belonging to this group.

B. The Bronze age

The largest and most famous centres of Argolis prospered during the so-called B r o n z e a g e, whose latter part was called the M y c e n a e a n a g e, for the entire area of continental Greece, (after the most representative argolid centre of that era).

The terms "Helladic era" is preferable when mention is made of the bronze age in connection with continental Greece, and "Minoan age" when mention of Crete is made. When dating artifacts, or remains of edifices, it is preferable to use these terms and their sub-divisions rather than specific dates because the latter cannot be fixed absolutely, but follow the progress and evidence of current research in archaeology. Classification of prehistoric remains, according to stratographic evidence, or according to specific characteristics of a given period and its sub-divisions, is safer and a more stable system.

The beginning of the third millennium B.C. has been accepted as the beginning of the H e l l a d i c or B r o n z e age, and its termination has been determined at the end of the 12th century B.C., or later, in other words, at a time when iron was used on a larger scale. This period has been sub-divided into smaller units of time as follows:

1) Early Helladic (EH) 3000-2800 to 2200 or 2000 B.C.
2) Middle Helladic (MH) 2200 or 2000 to 1600 B.C.
3) Late Helladic (LH) 1600 to 1100, or 1080 B.C.

The L a t e H e l l a d i c, or Mycenaean period has been subdivided into three chronological periods as follows:

1) First period (LH I) 1600-1500 B.C.
2) Second period (LH II) 1500-1400 B.C.
3) Third period (LH III) 1400-1100 or 1080 B.C.

5

The period of the greatest prosperity and renown of Mycenae coincides with the Late Helladic II and III. The latter period (LH III) has been sub-divided as follows:

1) First part of LH III (LH IIIa) 1400-1300 B.C.
2) Second part of LH III (LH IIIb) 1300-1200 B.C.
3) Third part of LH III (LH IIIc) 1200-1100, or 1080 B.C.

Using this chronological scale as a starting point, a number of outstanding stages mark the past of Argolis during the helladic period.

The oldest edifices worth mentioning on the acropolis of Mycenae and Tiryns belong to the Early Helladic period (in the middle, or even before the middle of the 3rd millennium B.C.).

The large circular structure (the one on the site of the megaron) on the acropolis of Tiryns was built during the Early Helladic period.

The most significant early helladic settlement was discovered in Lerna. Rectangular houses (and later on some with a rectangular and apsidal floor plan) were located on the low coastal hill, during the middle of this period, along with massive fortifications (a wall with towers). The exceptionally large house with the straight walls (the "house of tiles") was built during the early helladic period, as well.

Other early helladic settlements have been identified with certainty in the area of Prosymna (early helladic potsherds and statuettes have been unearthed during excavations at the Heraeum), in Midea (by the village of Dendra where early helladic potsherds and floors of houses were uncovered), in Argos (early helladic burials), in Kephalari (potsherds), in Asine (early helladic potsherds and statuettes), and near the Asclepieion of Epidaurus (early helladic potsherds were unearthed on the site of the shrine of Maleatas).

During the Middle Helladic period a palace was located at the top of the hill of Mycenae, along with a cemetery on the southwest slope. The royal shaft graves of Grave Circle B were used originally at the end of this period (around 1600 B.C.).

While Tiryns is only slightly represented during the middle helladic period (it is possible that the settlement went through a period of decline), Lerna, on the other hand, has quite a few remains of houses in evidence.

Argos was one of the most significant centres of Argolis during the middle helladic period. Houses, along with a fortified enclosure, were located on the hill of Deiras. Potsherds of the same period are to be found on the hill of Larissa, and extend over the entire area of the contemporary town.

The royal mycenaean graves of Grave Circle A (those inside the walls) have been dated in the beginning of the Late Helladic period (LH I). This very same enclosure which consists of a double circular row of upright stone slabs, was constructed at a later date. The construction of the graves of Grave Circle B (those outside the walls) had begun before that of the graves in Grave Circle A. Enclosure B was in use concurrently with Grave Circle A for 50 years, at least. It ceased being used, however, approximately 50 years before Grave Circle A finally stopped being used, as well.

The shaft-grave civilization of Mycenae, which lasted a century and a half, was the one which felt the strongest impact of the civilization of minoan Crete. This influence, however, slowed-down after 1450, resulting, after 1400, in the evolution of mycenaean art independently of any foreign influence (this is apparent in pottery making and the paintings on pottery).

The two centuries between 1400 and 1200 B.C. represent the peak of the Mycenaean civilization.

The tholos tombs, which are more recent than the shaft graves of the two grave circles, have been dated between 1500 and 1250 B.C.

The most significant buildings on the acropolis of Mycenae (that is, the walls with the lion gate, the palace at the top of the hill, and the courtyard in front of the megaron, along with the surrounding structures) have been dated from 1350-1325 B.C. (Wace). The Grand stone Staircase, which led to the courtyard, supposedly was completed at the end of the 13th century. The so-called "granary" was constructed during the LH IIIb period. The entire northeast extension of the walls, along with the secret cistern and the small exit to the south, are contemporary with the grand Staircase. In an attempt to synchronize the myths with archaeological evidence, the dating of the lion gate and the palace have been assumed as being more recent by one century: they are the works of Atreus (Agamemnon's father) who had built these structures around 1250 B.C. He had also constructed the "Treasury of Atreus" (G. Mylonas).

In Tiryns, the so-called "first acropolis" (the one with the entrance located in the large, or exterior propylon which was of a later date) was built shortly before the end of the LH II period (before 1420 B.C.). The "second acropolis" (which had an entrance located further out, between the two tall branches of the fortification wall) was constructed during the LH IIIa period. The "third acropolis", that is, the one extant today, was constructed at the end of the LH IIIb period which coincides with the end of the 13th century.

A wealth of remains of the Late Helladic period are to be found at the site of the contemporary town of Argos, as well as on the acropoleis of Larissa and Deiras. Rectangular shaft graves of the Late Helladic period were also excavated in Lerna, while in Asine a number of chamber tombs were found along with the former type. Similar types of graves have also been discovered in other mycenaean sites, such as Prosymna, Midea, and Nauplia.

C. Historical period

Archaeological evidence has led to the conclusion that the palace of Tiryns was still in use as a house until 750 B.C. approximately, even after the destruction of the mycenaean acropolis. It was restored later on and used as a temple dedicated to Hera (irrefutable literary evidence exists concerning the worship of Hera in Tiryns). Early inscriptions in Tiryns refer to the existence of another shrine dedicated to Athena.

During the geometric period, a temple dedicated to Hera, and certainly not to Athena, was constructed at the top of the hill of Mycenae.

The most important and largest shrine of Hera, however, was located in Prosymna (a town in the neighbourhood of Mycenae) where it acquired panhellenic fame, especially when, in later years, it came under the jurisdiction of Argos.

The leading role of Argos in Argolis begins in the 7th century B.C., under the leadership of Pheidon.

By then, Mycenae and Tiryns were small towns, having preserved, however, a certain degree of autonomy. The relative prosperity of archaic Tiryns can be substantiated from the inscriptions that were found engraved on the large stones of the galleries which led to the subterranean water-cisterns, near the northwest corner of the fortified enclosure (these inscriptions have been dated around 600 B.C.). It is known that Mycenae had sent 80 "hoplites" (heavily armed soldiers) to fight alongside Leonidas in Thermopylae, while the following year, along with Tiryns, 400 "hoplites" were sent to Plataia. Being unwilling to fight by the side of the Spartans, the Argives remained neutral during the war against the Persians.

Following the persian wars, the Argives could not tolerate any friends of the Spartans in their immediate vicinity, and used to punish the cities or towns that "had gone against" their will. As a consequence, in 468 B.C., they destroyed Mycenae and Tiryns. Later on Mycenae survived as a town "kome" that was directly connected with Argos. Tiryns was abandoned completely (at least immediately after its destruction), and its inhabitants settled in the coastal town of Halieis (across contemporary Portocheli).

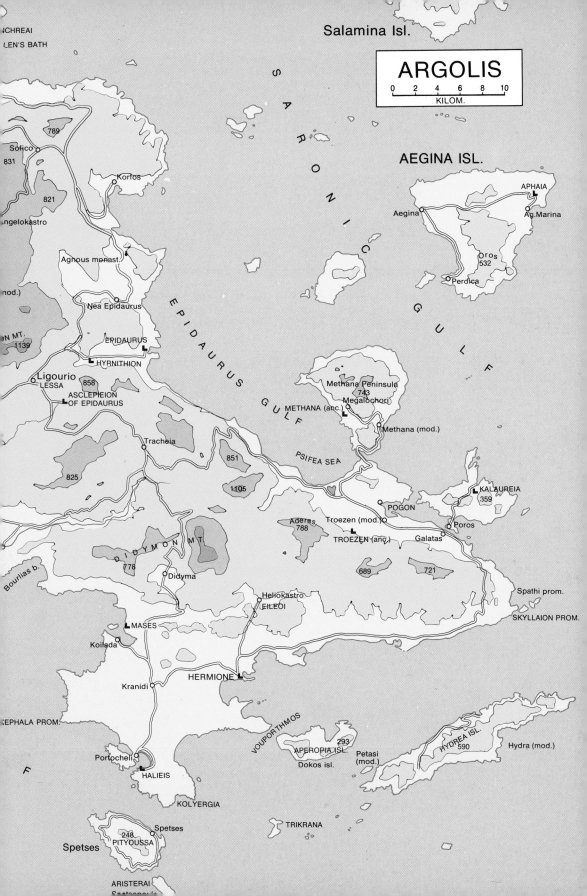

Salamina Isl.

ARGOLIS

0 2 4 6 8 10
KILOM.

AEGINA ISL.

CHREAI
LEN'S BATH

789

Sofico

831

Kortos

821

ngelokastro

mod.)

Agnous monast.

Nea Epidaurus

EPIDAURUS

HYRNITHION

ON MT.
1139

Ligourio
LESSA

858

ASCLEPIEION
OF EPIDAURUS

Tracheia

851

825

1105

S A R O N I C   G U L F

E P I D A U R U S   G U L F

PSIFEA SEA

AEGINA

APHAIA

Aegina

Ag. Marina

Oros
532

Perdica

Methana Peninsula
743
Megalochori

METHANA (anc.)

Methana (mod.)

KALAUREIA
359

POGON

Poros

Aderes
788

Troezen (mod.)

TROEZEN (anc.)

Galatas

689

721

Spathi prom.

SKYLLAION PROM.

Bourlias b.

D I D Y M O N   M T.

778

Didyma

Heliokastro
EILEOI

MASES

Koilada

Kranidi

HERMIONE

KEPHALA PROM.

F

Portocheli

HALIEIS

KOLYERGIA

VOUPORTHMOS

293
APEROPIA ISL.

Dokos isl.

Petasi
(mod.)

HYDREA ISL.
590

Hydra (mod.)

TRIKRANA

Spetses

248
PITYOUSSA

Spetses

ARISTERAI

1. Wild-boar hunt; a fresco from Tiryns.

2. Mycenaean lady holding a "pyxis" (a wooden box); a fresco from Tiryns.

I. MYTHICAL AND HISTORICAL ARGOLIS

1. Its Wealth of Traditions

No other site in the Peloponnese, or elsewhere in Greece is as rich in traditions as Argolis. Pindar called it "Argos, the home of Hera, home meet for a goddess; for it is lit up with countless distinctions by reason of deeds of prowess" (Nem. 10, 2 et seq.). The mountain ridges that surround this legendary plain 17-18 kilometres long, and of a much narrower width — still bear the visible signs of prehistoric Argos "which was grazed by horses"; of Tiryns, the high-walled, of "the rich in gold" Mycenae with the foundations of the tragic palace of the Atreides, who lived like brave knights and army leaders alongside their proud queens, preys of an indomitable hatred, as well as arrogant princes and princesses whose fateful actions, as these were described in the 5th century tragedies, revealed, first to the land of Greece, and eventually to the entire world, the tumultuous tyranny of a "baneful curse".

1

Neighbouring Corinth, of the Bacchiad and Kypselid families, soon felt how impoverished she was with regards to a glorious ancestry. Periander who was a Kypselid, and the Bacchiad poet Eumelos before him, both living in days not only of economic, but of intellectual, and artistic prosperity and bloom, could therefore, not tolerate the title of nobility which Homer had recognized and attributed to Corinth, presenting it (even though it is "wealthy") as a simple provincial centre which along with other peloponnesian cities, some of them quite insignificant towns, had participated in the Trojan War under the orders of the mycenaean king (B 570). Eumelos took it upon himself to enrich the mythical past of Corinth, identifying it with one of the Ephyres, and claiming the story of king Sisyphos, and the Sisyphides (Glaukus and Bellerophontes) for Corinth. Homer knew Sisyphos' Ephyra, deep in the recess of the Argolid plain (in the interior of Argos, which was grazed by horses, Z 152), and, consequently was a neighbour of Mycenae, since he had defined the site of the latter with the same expression (Odyss. γ 263). According to the Iliad, in spite of the fact that the Aiolian rulers of Ephyra carried on relations not only with aiolic Corinth, but with the Achaians of Argos as well, Glaukus was "an old hereditary friend" of Diomedes, king of Argos (Z 215), while his son, the noble Bellerophontes, with "beauty and manly loveliness" had charmed Anteia, wife of Proitos, king of Tiryns, thus compelling Proitos to send him to Lycia, and prepare involuntarily, a brilliant future for him (Z 168 et seq.). If, as many scholars believe, Ephyra of the Sisyphides was prehistoric Nemea (the hill of Tsougiza), or some other known prehistoric settlement in that area, it was located on the boundary line between Corinth and Argos, making it easy for the Corinthians of the historic era to appropriate its myths, as they had taken exclusive possession of other aiolic myths, (for instance, presenting Jason and Medea as rulers of Corinth).

2. The Mythical Past of Argolis in Relation to Data from Excavations

In Argolis, many prehistoric cities are known, either through tradition, or through archaeological excavations. Most legends are associated with three of them (Mycenae, Tiryns, and Argos). If excavations are able to shed any light in the hazy legends of the myths, one must deduce that, during neolithic times (at the beginning of the 3rd millennium B.C.), there was a settlement at Tiryns and Mycenae, while, regarding Argos its settlement is certain at approximately the middle of the same millennium (the early-helladic period, which has given us finds in the other two sites, as well). It would seem, however, true that during the middle-helladic period (after the year 2000 B.C.), Argos was superior to the other two because, aside from the numerous potsherds, excavations have brought to light the ruins of buildings and walls. This period is represented quite well in Tiryns, as well, but less so in Mycenae. Finally, during the late helladic period (1600-1100 B.C.), Mycenae assumes the leadership over the two other sites, not only by reason of its fortifications, but, also, by being a rich city. Tiryns distinguished itself towards the end of this period, following the extension of its fortified enclosure, when it acquired a fort comparable to that of Mycenae. When they invaded Argolis, the Dorians were faced with conditions as described above. During their long-term push towards the south, the Dorians had never encountered such forts as those of Mycenae and Tiryns. It is known that they did not invade the Peloponnese through the Isthmus of Corinth, but from the channel of Rion-Antirrion, from which point they advanced on Achaïa, Elis, and Arcadia without encountering opposition. Using Arcadia as their base of operations, they occupied Argolis. The sites of Mycenae and Tiryns were considered unfit, so Argos, which in the future, was definitely destined to become a city superior to all the other cities of Argolis, was chosen as their new base of

operations. In later years, the Greeks retained the memory of a historical event, that being the occupation of Corinth, with Argos as their point of departure; the Dorians had set-up camp at the Solygios hill (to the south of Kenchreais), and, after continuous attacks, they overcame the Aiolians of Corinth, whom they managed to turn into Dorians within the following two centuries (Thuc. 4, 42).

It is obvious that the local myths, which present Argos as the most ancient city of that area, and, simultaneously, as the most significant one, took into account only the final stages of its glory, and considered those as the original, or permanent state of affairs since the beginning of life in that area. These myths were all created after the merging of the Dorians with the older, local inhabitants, which began during the more advanced sub-mycenaean period and was completed during the geometric period. According to the final form which these myths took, and were then handed down as the early past of this land, the Pelasgians, with Inachos as their king, were the most ancient inhabitants of Argolis. Like all inhabitants of other lands, at first, the Pelasgians had no great political centre (city). The son of Inachos, Phoroneus, founded Argos, the first city in the world, which during antiquity was called the "phoronican city". Before Phoroneus' time people used to live in small settlements, or as nomads (Paus. 2, 15, 5). Phoroneus named his own son (Argos) after the city. This royal dynasty perpetuated itself through Argos, his two sons Peirasos and Phorbas, the latter's son Triopas, the sons of Triopas, Iasos and

Agenor, Agenor's son Krotopos, his son Sthenelas and Sthenelas' son Ghelanor (Paus. 2,16, 1). During the latter's reign, a distant relative, (a descendant of Ios, daughter of Iasos), and his daughters, (the Danaïds), arrived in Argos from Egypt, and succeeded Ghelanor to the throne. Following the death of Danaos, royal authority was passed on to Lygeus, the husband of the Danaïd Hypermestra. Throughout the entire area of Argolis, Lygeus was succeeded by his son, Abas, the father of Akrisios and Proitos who, following their father's death, divided the land between them. Akrisios reigned in Argos, and Proitos in Tiryns. Danae was Akrisios' daughter, and the mother of Perseus, the founder of Mycenae. So, it turns out that Mycenae is the last city of the three great cities of the Argolid plain. No memories of an older habitation (before Perseus) in Mycenae, have survived from the era when the various myths were created. After the reign of Perseus, his son, Sthenelos, reigned in Mycenae, while Sthenelos' son, Eurystheus, reigned in Tiryns. In the meantime, having being driven away by Pelops who was their father, and king of Elis, his sons, the Pelopids Atreus and Thyestes, arrived in Argolis, and the throne of Mycenae was taken over by them, and later on by Agamemnon, the son of Atreus. Following the death of its king Kylarabes, a descendant of Proitos, Orestes, Agamemnon's son, married Hermione, Helen's daughter, and annexed Sparta to his possessions in his role as Menelaos' successor, retaining Argos as his capital. Orestes' son, Tisamenos, succeeded him over the joint dominion, clashed with the invading Dorians and was defeated.

According to the myths, this was the past of Argolis until the Dorians became the new masters of the land, setting into motion a new period of prosperity, and renown for Argos, which had no rival to contend with in its role as a leading city. The myths reveal three pre-doric dynasties (that of Inachos, Danaos, and Atreus), with approximately twenty reigning kings altogether. The total time during which these kings reigned could not have been more than 600-700 years, in other words it is impossible to reach back before 1800 B.C., while excavations and dating of known evidence of life in this area begins in the early third millennium, not only in Mycenae and Tiryns but in a multitude of other sites in Argolis. The myths begin with the Pelasgians who were indo-european people, related to the Greeks, with whom they intermingled, and were assimilated (although, it seems that in certain areas, they retained their ethnic character, and probably their language, as well, until the early

4

historical period). They inhabited all of Greece, and especially Thessaly, the area around Larissa, which retained its name "Pelasgis" until historical times, and Arcadia where, according to local myths, their early ancestor, Pelasgos, had lived. The myths of Arcadia relate that Pelasgos was the first to teach people how to eat the fruit of the tame oak-tree, the acorn, as their food, instead of the usual common greens they had been eating, and to wear sheep-skins to protect their bodies from the cold (Paus. 8, 1, 5). This could only have taken place before the introduction of the cultivation of cereals (concerning Greece, this must have been before the 6th millennium). It is not possible, however, to base theories on chronology on these myths because many Arcadians used to eat acorns, as late as the historical period, and they might have enjoyed attributing their way of life to their venerable ancestor. The myths concerning Danaos, the head of the second argive dynasty, may echo a victorious landing and settlement of the argolid shores by a group of invaders from Egypt. The assimilation, however, of these invaders with the other Argives, was so complete that, in the Iliad, the appelations "Argives" and "Danaoi" had become identical, and were not only attributed to those who came from Argolis, but to all those coming from the rest of Greece, as well, along with the name Achaians. During the mycenaean period, the Achaians of Argolis constituted another segment of the population, probably the most significant one, supposedly originating, along with

5

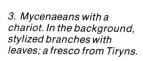

3. Mycenaeans with a chariot. In the background, stylized branches with leaves; a fresco from Tiryns.

4. A series of figure-eight mycenaean shields. This fresco from Tiryns, along with the three previous ones, has been restored with the help of extant pieces.

5. "Rhyton" (a libation cup) in the shape of a bull's head with gilded horns and a golden rosette on the forehead.

6. Segment of a fresco from the 13th century megaron of Mycenae.

6

the Acnaians of Lakonia, in the area which, during historical times, was called Phthiotis-Achaïa of Thessaly. According to mythology, Atreus, the founder of the third argive dynasty, belonged to a foreign royal house, whose member, Pelops, a refugee from Phrygia of Asia Minor, married Hippodameia and became king of Elis. The descendants of Pelops, the Atreides of Argolis, and Lakonia, appear in the epic not only as full-fledged Greeks, but as the most significant Achaian leaders, as well.

No matter how small and precarious the value of the myths might be as a historical source, they, undoubtedly, do offer some valuable information as e.q. that, during the pre-dorian period, the social sub-stratum of Argolis was not pure. Among the settled races, the Achaians were the most numerous, and had among other things, enforced their own dialect, as well as many of their own forms of worship. Following the settlement of the Dorians, during the 11th century B.C., the achaian element began to lose its characteristic qualities quite rapidly, and the land gradually accepted the doric way of life. Two hundred years later, Argolis was considered the most compact dorian power in the Peloponnese, the reason being that this area had accepted the greatest number of alien doric elements. The myth of the "descent of the Heraklides" was created in Argos, recognizing the Tirynthian Herakles as head of the Dorians, and presenting his descendants (the Herakleides) as returning to Argolis, their p a t e r n a l   l a n d. According to this myth, the other two doric Peloponnesian nations (Lakonia and Messenia where Herakles plays a very minor role in their traditions) were of secondary importance, and had been conceded to the Herakleid Aristomachos' two younger sons, namely, Aristodemos (who ruled Lakonia), and Kresphontes (who ruled Messenia). Aristomachos was the grandson of Hyllas, son of Herakles. The main descendant of Aristomachos was Temenos, his first son, who took over Argolis. From his capital in Argos, Temenos ruled a nation equal to that of legendary Agamemnon. Herodotus handed down the tradition that, before their dispute with Sparta over boundary lines, the Argives dominated all of eastern Peloponnese, to the island of Kythera (1,82). So it would seem that the nation of Argos, during the reign of Temenos and his successors, reached the door-step of history with as much glory as an heir to Mycenae ought to possess. Graves of the geometric period, which were rich in vases, and were excavated in the city of Argos, leave no doubt as to the importance, prosperity, and renown of the city before the archaic period.

3. Historical Period

The first nine Temenid kings of Argos belong to the prehistoric era. According to an authenticated view (of Ephoros) which was preserved by Strabo (8, 358), Pheidon was the tenth king that followed Temenos on the throne. During his reign, Pheidon was the most powerful leader of the Peloponnese. He introduced weights and measures, and minted coins in the cities that he ruled and were under his immediate jurisdiction. Considering himself a descendant of Herakles, he demanded the control of the Games which the former had established, and, especially the Olympic Games. If he had been at the Altis in order to organize the games of the 28th Olympiad (668 B.C.), this fact dates the years when he reached the apex of his glory (Paus. 6, 22,2). Being Agariste's suitor, it is possible that Pheidon's grand-son, and not his son, as has been reported (Herod. 6, 127), had been accepted and treated as a guest at the court of Kleisthenes of Sikyon, around 575 B.C. This grand son of Pheidon, Meltas, was the last Temenid king of Argos (the demos removed him from office) (Paus. 2,19,2). During the years that followed, the noblemen which held the title of king in Argos until the period of the Persian Wars, did not administer any real power. During Pheidon's times, many cities had been compelled to cooperate politically with him (Epidaurus, Troezen, Hermione, Aegina, Phleious, Kleonai, Sikyon). These cities and many others, which feared the pressure Pheidon, or his descendants could exert on them, opposed Argos (Herodotus refers to the opposition of the tyrant of Sikyon, Kleisthenes, which was quite strong, 5, 67-68). Many scholars believe that the amphictyony of Kalaureia, which was supposedly founded in 650 B.C., or a few years before, was the work of Aegina and those cities that wished to oppose the expansionary tendencies of Pheidon and the other Temenid leaders of Argos. The cities which formed a union for this purpose were not only those neighbouring Argos, such as Nauplia, Epidaurus, Hermione, Aegina, but Athens, as well as Prasiai (along the shore of Leonidion), and even Orchomenos (rather the arcadian and not the "minyeian" as stated by Strabo 8, 373).

During this same period, having secured its domination over Lakonia and Messenia, the second doric state (that of Sparta), started expanding along its northern borders, and found itself up against Argos. An earlier boundary dispute with Argos, which had started during Pheidon's era, was the occupation of the plain of Kynouria which lasted many centuries, during which the disputed area changed from one master to another. One of the oldest victories of the Argives against the Lakedaimonians was won at Hysiai (contemporary Achladokampos) in 699 B.C. (Paus. 2, 27,7). The defeated Spartans were quite obstinate and, after twenty years, won a decisive battle against the Argives near Thyrea (in 547 B.C., Herod. 1, 82). This victory was the one which opened the road to the domination and leading role Sparta was to play in the Peloponnese. The Spartan army could reach quite close to Argos, without any fear. In 494 B.C., during the famous battle of Sepeia (near Tiryns) Kleomenes, the king of Sparta, annihilated all the able-bodied Argive soldiers, creating a situation whereby the slaves of Argos, those who had occupied Tiryns when driven away (Herod. 6, 76-83), were obliged, for a number of years, to administer the government. As a result, during the Persian Wars which followed (490-479 B.C.), Argos was exhausted and remained neutral, avoiding a military coalition with Sparta during that crucial period. As opposed to this, the towns of Mycenae and Tiryns, which, by then had declined considerably, were able to send an army to Plataia, which was to fight alongside the Spartans who were the leaders of all the greek forces in that location. Due to the fact that these two cities continued having friendly relations with Sparta, they found themselves in a position of intense antagonism with the Argives, who, in 468, destroyed both towns. Most of the

7. Pottery from Grave Circle B in Mycenae (outside the Lion Gate). It has the shape of a duck, and was carved out of rock-crystal at approximately 1530 B.C.

inhabitants were expatriated. Those who, in later years, continued living there formed the two unwalled villages, "komae", of Argos. In order to fight against the Spartans more effectively, following the persian wars, the Argives formed an alliance with the Athenians(461 B.C.), and were able, the following year, to beat them in Oinoe, an argive town which was reached by the spartan army through the mountain passes of Mount Artemission.

Argos did not participate in the Peloponnesian League during the peloponnesian war, and tried to remain far from the conflicting parties. Shortly after the peace of Nikias, however, it allied itself with the Athenians and clashed with the Spartans in Mantineia in 418 B.C. The Mantineians and the Eleians were also on the Argive side, but the Spartans and their allies were victorious. The following year, the Argives began to build their long walls from Argos to Temenion (between Nauplia and Lerna), in order to communicate unimpeded with their athenian allies. The timely intervention of the Spartans put an end to this building enterprise.

During the corinthian war (395-386 B.C.), the Argives and the Corinthians were closely bound by a military and political coalition, and the argive forces, which had camped permanently in Corinth, faced Agesilaos along with the corinthian army and the athenian expeditionary corps under Iphikrates.

During the Macedonian and Roman period, Argos was one of the most thriving peloponnesian cities, never again reaching, however, the stage of glory it had acquired during the pre-historic or the archaic period. The epirote king, Pyrros, clashed near Argos with the king of Macedonia, Antigonos Gonatas, and beat him in 275 B.C. Chasing the defeated army, however, through the streets of Argos, a tile, which had been thrown from above by an argive woman, as rumour has it, hit him on the head and killed him. He was buried in the enclosure of the shrine of Demetra (Paus. 1, 13, 8). In 229 B.C., Argos became a member of the Achaic Confederation (the coins that were minted at that date bear the inscription "Achaeans' Argives").

Following the defeat of the confederate army by the Romans in 146 B.C., Argos was subjugated to them, not suffering, however, the harsh punishment which Mommios held in store for Corinth, the centre of the anti-roman activities of the confederation. As can be witnessed by the ruins of buildings, sculptured decorations and paintings which were revealed during excavations, Argos lived through a period of financial prosperity during roman times. In the interval between the destruction of Corinth and before its reconstruction, which began in 44 B.C., Argos was the second city in the Peloponnese after Sparta (Strab. 8, 377). One hundred, or one hundred and fifty years later, the reconstructed city of Corinth assumed the leadership once more.

II. TOPOGRAPHICAL SURVEY OF ANCIENT ARGOLIS

Before going into the details of excavations at the better known sites of Argolis (Mycenae, the Heraion of Argos, Argos, Tiryns, and the Asclepieion of Epidaurus) a list is presented, and a brief legend of each ancient site, where ruins have been preserved, is given. The sites are named in the order in which one approaches each along the contemporary routes and roads, or after short side trips from the main arteries.

1. Boundaries of Ancient Argolis. Bordering Corinthian Sites

The hills of T r e t o s (above Dervenakia) constituted the northern, and the fertile T h y r e a t i s (the plain of Astros) constituted the southern borders of the land. It was separated from Arcadia by the mountains of Lyrkeion, Artemission, and Parthenion.

He who headed from Corinth to Argolis, would come across the last towns of Corinth, before the Dervenakia pass, at the site of present-day Aghios Vassileios. The city of T e n e a, where one comes across a few remains of buildings (from the fortification walls and houses), is located between the villages of Chiliomodi and Klenia. Graves have been excavated there, as well.

At the site of Z y g o u r i e s, near the railway station of Aghios Vassileios, a prehistoric settlement has been excavated, which might have been that of ancient Kleones. The foundations of H e r a k l e i o n (the shrine of Herakles in Kleones) were excavated to the right of the road to Nemea, before the rise which leads to Kontostavlos. According to the myths, two feats of Herakles are associated with this area; the death of Kteates and Eurytos, who had treated the hero dishonourably in the past, and the slaying of the lion of Nemea, whose lair was located among the hills of Tretos. Humble remains of the walls and the acropolis of K l e o n e s are located a short distance to the north of Herakleion.

Past the hills of the village of Kontostavlos (officially known as Kleones in the present), the road runs downhill towards ancient N e m e a, where the remains of the temple of Zeus have been preserved, and, following the cleaning of the ruins, stand quite imposing. Excavations are still going on at present in areas adjoining the temple, such as the stadium, where the panhellenic games, Nemeia, used to take place. Originally, Nemea belonged to Kleones, which used to conduct the games, but later on this organization of the games was taken over by Argos.

To the west of ancient Nemea, the same road leads to contemporary Nemea (Aghios Georgios), and within a short distance to the northwest, to the ruins of ancient P h l e i o u s. The theatre and the public buildings of the agora are being excavated at present. Phleious of antiquity was associated with Sparta through steadfast ties of friendship, rather than to its neighbouring city of Argos.

2. Ancient and Contemporary Road-Approaches from Corinth

In antiquity, whoever started out for Argos from Corinth (contemporary Old Corinth) used to pass Akrocorinth on the right (today one passes on the left), and would reach Kleones first. He could, then, enter the narrow pass of Dervenakia (where the railway and the main road pass), and proceed towards Argos, leaving Mycenae to the left. If one wished to avoid Dervenakia, one could take the mountain-road which used to be called K o n t o p o r i a , and is practically identical with the present country road of Chiliomodi-Klenia-Aghionoros (with the impressive ruins of the late-byzantine fort) -Limnes-contemporary Prosymna-Chonika-Argos. In order to guard this road, a s i n g l e f o r t, which is extant in all its height, a short distance to the right of the contemporary main road, had been built by the Argives (probably during macedonian times). The fort is visible as soon as the road passes through Dervenakia.

The ancient main road, like the contemporary one, used to wind through the pass of Dervenakia, but in order to reach Argos, it followed a course closer to Mycenae, ancient Prosymna, and the Heraion.

3. Ancient Sites to the Southwest of Argos

Another road, of a southwest orientation, led from Argos to Arcadia, through the heights of Parthenion. On the way, a short distance from Argos, one came across the spring of Erasinos (the Kephalari of today), and further on, across one of the p y r a m i d s of Argos, at the contemporary village of Hellenikon (a short distance to the southwest of Kephalari). The pyramid, which during late antiquity was considered a grave monument (a common burial place), known today to have been a fort, is extant to a considerable height (see plate 10). A room, which is practically square in the interior, has sides 7 metres long. This is similar to the egyptian pyramids, in that, on the exterior, the four walls of the building converge towards the centre.

Caves (which have been embodied in its adjoining buildings) can be seen at Kephalari, at the site of the church, next to the fountain-head of Erasinos. Recent excavations in the caves have brought to light the fact that these had been inhabited, not only during the neolithic, but during the mesolithic period, as well.

The ancient approach to arcadian Tegea left the spring of Erasinos to the right, the pyramid to the left and wound uphill, among inaccessible heights, towards the contemporary village of Achladokampos. The ancient town of H y s i a i, which constituted the last western argive settlement, was located only a short distance before Achladokampos. Just outside Achladokampos, practically at the foot of the village, the main highway reaches the ruins of the walls of Hysiai which are located on a small hill, its acropolis, near a church and a spring of water that runs along the roadside.

4. Ancient Sites to the Northwest of Argos

Upon taking the other road to the north of Argos, and following a northwest direction (parallel to the river-bed of Inachos), one would reach the two towns,

Lyrkeia and Ornees, that bordered Argos. L y r k e i a had already been identified long ago with the ruins of fortification walls on the hill, located just outside the village of Kato Belessi, which is officially called Lyrkeia today. Certain scholars have identified ancient Lyrkeia with the ruins near the village of Sterna, and others still, with those at Schinochori. According to tradition, in order to avoid the pursuit and capture by Danaos, Lyngeus took refuge in Lyrkeia. The safest site, however, would have been "Kastraki" of Kato Belessi which is linked with high mountains, and would have enabled him to observe the messages that Hypermestra sent him by lighting fires at the top of the Larissa of Argos. The walls of Kastraki belong to post-classical times, but potsherds of the helladic period have been found on the site.

The town of O r n e a i was located farther to the north, near the village Gymno (on the road from Sterna to Nemea), or, according to a more probable version, near neighbouring Leonti.

If one follows the contemporary road, which runs practically parallel to the bed of the river Charadros (the Xerias of today), one reaches south of Schinochori, among the first rises of Artemission, the village of Mazi (called Aria today). It is believed that ancient O i n o e, known from the military clash of the Argives and the Athenians against the Lakedaimonians in 460 B.C. (see p. 19 above), which took place near this village, was located on this site.

5. Ancient Sites to the East of Argos

Following an easterly course, the road from Argos to Arachnaion leaves the village Dendra, which has been renamed Midea, to the left. The mycenaean city of M i d e a, where many tholos and chamber tombs have been excavated, was located a short distance to the north. A bronze suit of armour (see plate 9) was found recently in one of them. The Cyclopean walls of Midea have been preserved on a hill above Dendra.

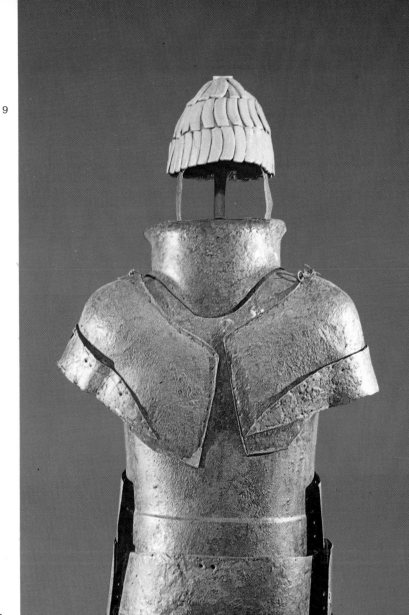

8. Part of the fortified
enclosure of the ancient
town at Kastraki, Kato
Belessi. This town has been
identified with the ancient
town of Lyrkeia (see p. 22).

9. Bronze mycenaean
breast-plate from the
village of Dendra (east of
Argos) where the
mycenaean city of Midea
was located. Four wide
bronze plates were used for
the protection of the body,
from the hips to the neck.
One for the neck and two
more for over the
shoulders. A helmet, made
of wild-boar tusks, has been
placed over the breast-
plate.

6. The Road to Nauplion - Epidaurus. Ancient Epidauria

If one takes the main road from Nauplion to Ligourio and the Asklepieion of Epidaurus, one leaves the village of Aghios Demetrios, or Metochi to the left. A fort of the 4th century B.C., which was built by the Argives for the purpose of controlling the road to Epidaurus, has been preserved at the top of the hill, a short distance to the west of this village. The fort is known by the name of K a z a r m a, and is often identified with the ancient city of Lessa, where it is known that a temple of Athena had been located in antiquity (concerning views on the location of Lessa, read below). At the foot of the hill below Kazarma, exactly at the left side of the road, a tholos mycenaean tomb was excavated recently.

A b r i d g e, which has been built with blocks from the walls of Tiryns, and has been covered with a corbelled pointed arch, like the galleries of Tiryns, is extant in very good condition today, to the left of the road, just before the tholos grave of Kazarma. The bridge is considered mycenaean. The road that passes over it is still in use today, exactly as it used to be in antiquity.

Before the road reaches Ligourio, it leaves the village K a s t r a k i some distance to the left. Another fortified site, similar to Kazarma, but somewhat smaller in size, is located near this village. Certain scholars have identified Lessa at this site, without substantial evidence, however.

A great deal closer to Ligourio, near the church of St. Marina, practically at the outskirts of the village, on a site that is visible to the left of the main road, the ruins of another pyramid, which is in a worse state of preservation than the one at Hellenikon, are to be found. One corner, along with a small part of the two sides,

10. An argive Pyramid located near the village Hellenikon, to the southwest of Kephalari. It had been considered a "polyandrion", but could also have been a fort used to control the road to Hysiai (Achladokampos) and Tegea.

11. Kephalari, near Argos. The church has been constructed near caves which had been inhabited during the prehistoric period. The river, Erasinos, springs from the ground under the caves and the church.

12. A wall on the acropolis of ancient Epidaurus.

13. A tower of the argive fort at Kazarma; on the road from Argos to Epidaurus.

14. A bridge dated in the mycenaean period. It is constructed in a simple corbelled pointed arch of large blocks of stone, similar to the galleries of Tiryns.

whose inward convergence is quite evident, are the only extant parts of this building.

As far as one can deduce from potsherds of the classical period, traces of a fortification wall, and from blocks of stone with sculptured reliefs which have been immured in church-walls, it is certain that a small ancient town must have existed in Ligourio. Perirrhanteria (holy water fonts) were found as well, bearing votive inscriptions to Athena, a fact that allows one to deduce that L e s s a and the famous temple of the goddess, which was of great renown in antiquity, was located in Ligourio. This site had been inhabited during prehistoric times (recent excavations have revealed a mycenaean chamber tomb). The view that the boundary line between Argos and Epidaurus was located at the site of Lessa, at Ligourio, therefore, is thus further strengthened and substantiated.

Upon leaving Ligourio, a branch of the main road follows a southeastern direction and ends at the Asklepieion of Epidaurus (see p. 128 below), while another road takes a northeasterly direction and reaches Old Epidaurus, the town that occupies the site of a n c i e n t E p i d a u r u s, and has an exceptionally good harbour. The theatre of ancient Epidaurus (a smaller one than that at the Asklepieion) was excavated recently in that site. The fortification walls of its acropolis are extant over the theatre, from which the engraved stone benches had been removed and used as building material during the construction of the walls. Segments of the fortified enclosure of the city, which are of a more ancient date, are located on the adjoining peninsula to the east. The foundations of buildings which have been inundated by the sea, and are presently being studied for the first time, are still in existence today.

15. "Episkope", Troezen: Ruins on the site of the ancient shrine of Hippolytos.

7. Troezen

If, from the Asklepieion of Epidaurus, one follows a country road in a southerly direction, one will descend towards the shore of Troezen, having passed the village of Tracheia. Before one reaches contemporary Troezen, one comes upon a fork of the road towards Methana, with the sulphur springs of water. An asphalt mountain-road leads to Megalochori, and the eastern shore of the peninsula. The ancient c i t y o f M e t h a n a was located along the shore of Megalochori (a small settlement is located on the same site even today). Segments of the ancient fortification walls have been preserved along the sea-shore, and on a low hill which used to serve as its acropolis. These fortifications had been restored during medieval times. Segments of the medieval walls have been preserved, and have been superimposed upon the ancient parts of the wall.

Following the main road in a southerly direction, one leaves, to the left, the harbour of Troezen, Bidi, which was called P o g o n in antiquity, and to the right Troezen itself, (or Damala). Many segments of fortification walls, and the foundations of the temple of a n c i e n t T r o e z e n have been preserved in the contemporary town and its immediate environs. Many inscriptions, as well as sculptured members have been found here. Most of the architectural members were

preserved at the shrine of Hippolytos, a short distance to the northwest of the contemporary town (these are foundations of the temple of Hippolytos, and the structures that belonged to the Asklepieion that was located there, as well as ruins of altars and shrines). The ruins of the medieval church of the episcopate of Damala, from which the entire area has derived its name "Episkope", have been preserved to a considerable height. The site where, during the revolution the national assembly, which elected Kapodistrias as the governor of Greece in 1827, convened is located on the opposite side of the town, at the site of Phleba.

Leaving Troezen behind, the road descends towards the sea-shore, and reaches Galatas, a suburb of Poros, at the narrowest point of the channel. The town of Poros is located just across the channel, where an asphalt road leads to the naval training building, and hence to the northern shores of the island, via a recently paved mountain-road. The foundations of stoas, and other buildings of the famous shrine of P o s e i d o n o f Ka la u r e ia have been excavated at the site which is located, above a natural cove, quite high on the side of the mountain. The area where the shrine was located was the centre of one of the amphiktyonies of the peloponnesian cities which had been joined by Athens and Aegina. The c i t y o f Ka l a u r e i a, the capital of the island, was located at the same site, near the shrine of Poseidon.

16. The peninsula of Hermione: Ruins of the shrines of the ancient city.

8. Hermionis

Running along the eastern and southern shore of Hermionis, across from the islands of Hydra (ancient H y d r e a), and Dokos (ancient A p e r o p i a), the main road leads from Galatas to Hermione. The contemporary town is located at a deep recess of the cove. During the period of late antiquity, an ancient city by the same name, was located on the same site. Before that, however, it had spread towards the east, on the narrow peninsula. Segments of the ancient walls have been preserved along the shore of this peninsula, along with the foundations of a peripteros temple, and of another smaller one, in the area located in the middle. A segment of the fortification walls, which had been restored during medieval times, has been preserved close to the contemporary town. Large inscribed pedestals of statues and busts, which had been used as building material for the walls, have been preserved in situ.

A road towards the north ends in contemporary Heliokastro, the site of ancient E i l e o i, where the mountain-road connecting Troezen and Hermione used to pass in antiquity. A shrine of the eleusinian gods, Demetra and Kore, was in existence in Eileoi. Somewhat lower, by the shore, another shrine was dedicated to Demetra "thermasia" ("the T h e r m e s i o n"), in other words, to the goddess who insured the required heat for the growth of cereals, protecting them from frost. The name of a village by the shore, which is called Thermesia, and of cape Thermesi, remind one of that shrine.

From Hermione, another road leads to the west, towards Kranidi, the capital of the province of Hermionida. Hence, a road towards the south leads to Portocheli, with the secure natural cove to which it owes its name. The opening of the cove faces the southwest. As one enters this natural harbour one finds contemporary Portocheli to the left, and, to the right, the ruins of the ancient settlement by the

16

name of H a l i e i s, or H a l i k e. The ancient city had been built along the sea-shore, and was surrounded by walls which climbed the neighbouring hill where its acropolis used to be located. Parts of the walls and the buildings by the shore have been submerged in the sea. When, in 468 B.C., the Argives destroyed Tiryns (see p. 19 above), its inhabitants settled at Halieis, but continued calling themselves Tirynthians, as witnessed by the coins they minted in their new land. During the peloponnesian war, the few inhabitants of the small town of Halieis (who were called Halieis, or Halikoi, as well) allied themselves with the Spartans and, as a consequence, the city suffered frequent pillaging by the athenian navy.

The island of Spetses lies in front of the opening of the cove of Cheli. Its capital, by the same name, was inhabited in antiquity, as well. At A g. M a r i n a, a settlement of the helladic period has come to light during excavations. The ancient name of the island was n e s o s P i t y o u s a (pine-tree covered island). The island of Spetsopoula was called A r i s t e r a.

Another road to the north of Kranidi leads to two other villages of the same province, Koilada and Didyma. Ancient settlements also existed in the immediate area. Koilada is located to the right, as one sails into that cove. Ancient M a s e s used to be situated on the opposite shore (the one to the north). A medieval fort is still in evidence on the hill. Potsherds of the mycenaean period have been found in Mases which is mentioned by Homer (B 562). Inadequate, in number, and poor, architectural members of the city of the historical period are also in evidence. One also finds a cave, in the same area of the cove, which is known by the name of P h r a g t h i. Recent excavations have proven the existence of a settlement of the 8th century B.C., when the cultivation of cereals was unknown, and people lived by hunting, fishing, and the various fruit and nuts they gathered.

Finally, an ancient settlement, by the name of D i d y m o i, to which belonged the ancient architectural members, as well as a few inscriptions which were found on the site, had been built there, on the location of contemporary Didyma, so named after the "didyme" (twin) mountain-tops of that area.

17. Hellenistic fortifications in Asine.

18. A section of the large tower. Medieval walls in the background.

9. Asine

Following the road that leads from Nauplion to Tolo, and before reaching the latter, one passes through the contemporary village of Asine (former Jaferaga). Another road leads to a small seaside settlement of this village, where one can view the ruins of the walls and fortification towers of a n c i e n t A s i n e. Tolo lies a short distance to the southeast. Asine was a prehistoric city, which was known to Homer (B 560), as well, and occupies the top of the hill which rises precipitous from the sea. Excavations have revealed architectural ruins and graves belonging to all the periods of the bronze age. Along with mycenaean chamber tombs, other graves of later eras, up to the geometric period, as well as pottery were found in these graves. It has been assumed by scholars that most of the inhabitants of Asine had been forced, by the Argives, to abandon the city during the early years of the historical period. According to one view, the Spartans who had recently taken over Messenia, allowed them to settle on the shores of this land, which had been "taken by the force of spears", where the refugees founded messenian Asine. During the hellenistic period, argolid Asine became a thriving settlement once more, and was then fortified with the walls in evidence today. The location was considered a significant fort during medieval times, when the fortified enclosure was restored. In fact, in numerous sections, the ancient walls have been preserved at a higher level than the medieval superstructure.

10. Nauplia

The northern section of a small peninsula, at a deep recess of the gulf of Argolis, where contemporary Nauplion lies, used to be occupied, during the historic period, by a n c i e n t N a u p l i a. A rocky hill, which is 85 metres high, constitutes the southern section of this peninsula, which on the one hand slopes rather gently towards the inhabited section of the city, and, on the other, rises precipitous from the sea. This hill was used as the acropolis of ancient Nauplia (A k r o n a u p l i a). To the southeast, it adjoins a higher rocky hilltop, Palamidi, 216 metres heigh, which can be approached by a winding staircase whose 857 steps, in most cases, have been carved out of, but, at other cases, have been constructed on the rock. Evidence of life is certain from the 3rd millennium onward, but, at no time, during the pre-christian era was there any evidence of a significant settlement at this location. It is possible that Akronauplia had been fortified during mycenaean times; the settlement, however, was small in comparison to the neighbouring cities of Mycenae and Tiryns, a fact that becomes a certainty, when strengthened by the poor mycenaean graves which were excavated near Pronoia, at the foot of the hill. As a result, Homer does not mention Nauplia anywhere. In the middle of the 7th century B.C., Nauplia makes its appearance, for the first time, among the founding members of the amphiktyonies of Kalaureia (Strab. 8, 374). Before the end of the century, however, the Argives conquered the site and used it as their sea-port. The inhabitants of Nauplia voted along with them during the amphiktyonies. The ancient walls, which have been preserved on Akronauplia (below the medieval ones) are the work of Argives (a polygonal manner of construction with large blocks of stone, reminiscent of the walls of argive Larissa). Nauplia remained an insignificant town, even as the sea-port of Argos, and declined even further during the roman imperial era.

The golden age of this site began during medieval times, and especially during the Frankish occupation. During the first decades of the 13th century, along with other fortified sites of the Peloponnese, it had been overtaken by the Frankish leaders which had settled in parts of Greece following the fourth crusade. Within the century that followed, these people created the first fortified retreats of Argolis; namely, excluding Akronauplia, they provided for the first fortification or restoration of the old walls on the Larissa of Argos, at Asine, on the Pontinos hill of Lerna, and Thermesi of Hermionis. When the Venetians became the masters of Nauplion, at the end of the 14th century, they restored the fortification walls of Akronauplia, extended the defense walls of Palamidi, and fortified the small island of Bourdzi, which is located less than 500 metres from the jetty on the shore of Nauplion. These defensive works fell under Turkish attack of 1540, were re-conquered by the Venetians under Morozini, a century and a half later (in 1686), only to be occupied (29 years later) by the Turks once again.

Nauplion, or Anapli (as it was already being called during the late-byzantine period) was captured by the revolting Greeks during the second year of the revolution (shortly after the decisive victory at Dervenakia in 1822).

Ioannis Kapodistrias who, the previous year, had been elected governor at the national assembly of Troezen, disembarked at Nauplion in January, 1828. It became the capital of the new nation in 1829 (instead of Aegina). Kapodistrias was assassinated there two years later (1831), and in January 1833 king Otho arrived at the port of Nauplion followed by an escort of 36 foreign ships, and numerous attendants to the court. In July of the same year, it was decided to transfer the capital to Athens, a plan which was realized in 1834.

19. Modern Nauplion with its peninsula and the island of Bourdzi (aerial view).

20. Nauplion. During the medieval period, along with the fort on Akronauplia, Bourdzi secured a tight control of the harbour.

21. Nauplion. The fort of Palamidi.

22. A deep recess of the gulf of Argolis; view from Palamidi.

23. In 1834, a lion was carved in high relief on a niche of the rock which was smoothed out especially for that purpose. The site is located above Nauplion, and commemorates the death of King Otho's Bavarians who had died, at that time, in Nauplion and the surrounding countryside.

24. A venetian sculptured representation of a winged lion, the symbol of Mark, the evangelist, patron saint of Venice. He became the patron saint of the city, following the transport of his relics from Alexandria to Venice.

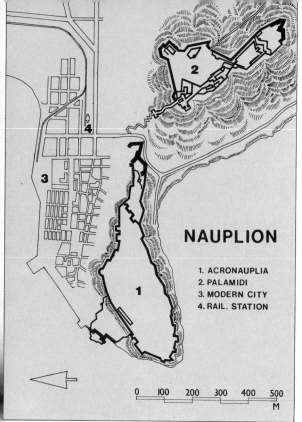

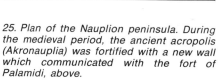

25

26

25. Plan of the Nauplion peninsula. During the medieval period, the ancient acropolis (Akronauplia) was fortified with a new wall which communicated with the fort of Palamidi, above.

26-27 View from Akronauplia: The plain of Argos, and the road from Argos to Nauplion. The gulf of Argolis, the seashore from Nauplion to Lerna, and the fortified island of Bourdzi to the left.

27

30

28. View from Akronauplia, towards the fortified island of Bourdzi.

29-30. The fort of Palamidi; the entrance and a view of the interior.

31

11. Lerna

Before the main asphalt road, and the railroad to Tripolis begin their ascent towards Achladokampos, both pass by the site of a n c i e n t L e r n a (the contemporary town of Myloi). A new asphalt road, running along the seashore, from Nauplion to Lerna has been put to use recently. Springs of plentiful water gush from the foot of P o n t i n o s h i l l, a short distance from the sea. In the past, this water was used to power many watermills which were located near the sea. The village of Myloi owes its name to these very mills. A smaller quantity of water runs into the sea. Since, at this point, the angle of the slope is insignificant, even today the water stagnates quite easily, before a river of sorts runs into the sea. As a result, a lake of a 60-metres perimeter has been formed. Its depth is considerable, and it has an

31. Remains of the early
helladic fortifications of
Lerna. The temporary
structures, erected for their
protection, are visible here,
along with the foundations
of two towers, on the left.

32. Excavated ruins of
buildings in the prehistoric
settlement of Lerna.

32

abundance of water-plants along its shores which used to form an obstruction to
any view of the bottom. In antiquity, this lake was called A l k y o n i a, and common
belief had it that no one could see its bottom or measure its depth. Lernaia Hydra, of
the myth, is said to have had its lair in one of the springs which was named
A m y m o n e.

The prehistoric settlement of Lerna, whose settlement begins in neolithic
times, and reaches the height of its prosperity during the early-helladic years (2500
B.C. and somewhat later), was excavated at this site, on a low rise of the ground near
the springs of water, a short distance from the sea. The houses have right-angle
floor-plans, and the settlement was adequately fortified. Besides sculptured
decorations and inscriptions of the hellenistic period of Lerna, prehistoric graves
were excavated outside this settlement, on the site of the contemporary village,
where the city of Lerna used to be located during the historical period.

33. Early-helladic hearth from Lerna, as reconstructed at the museum of Nauplion. An irregular circle of a 1,15-metre diameter, it bears incised decorative patterns on the brim. It was made out of clay, while a depression in the middle held the ashes. A theory has been put forth as to its being used in sacred household rituals (2500 B.C.).

34. Section of the fortified wall of the significant ancient town located on the hill of Hellenikon, to the right of the paved road between Astros and Agh. Petros, Kynourias.

12. Thyreatis

In antiquity one could descend from Lerna to the area of the Thyreatis plain (the one so often fought about) by following two courses; one, along the seashore which followed the eastern foothills of Zavitsa, a little higher than the contemporary main road of Myloi-Kiveri-Astros, and another, a more inaccessible mountain-road, which left the top of Zavitsa to the left and descended deep into the recesses of the plain. In antiquity, this second course was named A n i g r a i a. Today, the corresponding road starts just outside Myloi, leaves Kiveri to the left, and climbs the western heights of Zavitsa, to end at Kato Doliana, Loukou and Astros.

Thucydides knew only of two cities in Thyreatis, T h y r e a and A n t h e n e (5, 41). He states that, being a border area, this entire region was forever disputed over, both by the Argives and the Lakedaimonians. In his days, the Lakedaimonians had exclusive rights in the area, which they had handed over to the Aeginetes, who had been forced by the Athenians to leave Aegina. At the beginning of the peloponnesian war, when the Athenians raided the shores of the Peloponnese by sea, the Aeginetes of Thyrea, with the aid of the Spartans, began the hurried construction of a wall around the seaside settlement of Thyrea. Before the completion of the fortifications, however, the Athenians disembarked in that area, forcing the Aeginetes to secure themselves in the fortified "upper city" of Thyrea which was located at a distance of 10 stadia from the sea. The Athenians, however, went after them even there, and overran the city which they looted and burned (4, 57). This description is evidence enough for the identification of Thyrea, which was located by the sea, with contemporary Astros, where an incomplete fortification wall is to be found, one which gives the impression of truly having been built in haste. "Ano" (upper) Thyrea must be identified with the ancient fortified settlement of Hellenikon, a short distance to the west of Astros, but farther than it is referred to by Thucydides.

Herodotus knows this same region of Kynouria as being argive, having been won away from the Lakedaimonians, and reports that, a short time before the battle of Sepeia (see p. 18 above), Kleomenes had embarked in Thyrea with his army, and, then, had landed on the shore near Tiryns (6, 76). The fact that, beside the name of "Thyrei", he uses the plural "Thyreai" (1, 82), as well, demonstrates that he knew the upper settlement of Thyrea, which was the most significant, anyway.

The city of Anthene, as referred to by Thucydides, or Athene, (2,38,6) by Pausanias, must be identified with the second fortified city of Thyrea, also located on the shore, at the site of contemporary Agh. Andreas. Sections of an exceptionally well-constructed polygonal wall are in evidence there.

One other city, E u a, which is referred to during the period of late antiquity (from inscriptions of the same period we have the name of the demos Euitas), must have been located at the area of the convent of Loukou. This same convent had been built on the site of an Asklepieion of Eua. The Asklepiad Polemokrates, son of Machaon, (Paus. 2, 38, 6) was especially honoured in this Asklepieion. A large sculptured votive relief with Asklepiades, as well as a small segment of a marble statue of Asklepios (part of a staff with a coiled snake) come from the convent of Loukou. The athenian family of Herodus Atticus had special ties with this area, as a country-house of Herodes was located a short distance to the northeast of the "Polemokrateion".

III. EXCAVATIONS IN ARGOLIS

1. The History of the Excavations

The excavations in Argolis are the oldest that were ever conducted on greek soil. It is known that after 1870, scholars in the field of archaeology began to consider a closer contact with the remains of ancient life increasingly more necessary, and were not satisfied in depending exclusively on literary sources. In the past, excavations had been conducted in isolated instances only, and on a small scale, not because these had been demanded by an advanced level of research, but because treasures were sought after, or curiosity, and the emotion which one feels when one comes into immediate contact with a past, made famous by history, or poetry, had dictated them. The limited excavation of Pompey is an example of this trend. In 1748 this was dictated mainly by the curiosity which contemporary people felt about viewing the unaltered day-to-day life of a thriving centre of civilization which, in 79 A.D., had suddenly been covered by the ashes of the volcano.

This excavation which was conducted at various intervals, after the middle of the 18th century, aroused the visionary temperament of Heinrich Schliemann, as he himself used to say, and led him to the dedication of his life to one of the most legendary pages of the past. Schliemann became the pioneer of excavations and archaeological research in Greece. He did not begin with the intentions of shedding light on the problems of ancient history, or ancient art, but of satisfying his desire of finding extremely old artifacts. He would become quite emotional when holding a necklace which had been worn by a proud queen of Mycenae, or the sword which had been used by Agamemnon, or some other mycenaean ruler.

Schliemann had spent his childhood in the town of New Buckow in Mecklenburg (in northern Germany, close to Denmark), where his own father, a poor protestant priest, served as his first teacher, until he was nine years old. He planted a warm love of ancient history in his young son's mind, and taught him a little latin. Schliemann preferred ancient greek, and was unhappy that, not knowing any other ancient language, his father could not be of further assistance to him. He learned some ancient greek later on, while attending the first years of High School. He was soon compelled, however, to interrupt his studies and begin working at a grocery store, at the age of 14. During the interval he spent there, he was able to perfect his knowledge of ancient greek, to the point, where, according to his autobiography, he was able to recite complete passages from the Iliad, and the Odyssey "in rhyme". Following an accident he suffered before the age of twenty, he decided to work as a steward on board a ship. The ship was wrecked, however, and Schliemann who, by that time had six languages in his command—having a great facility in learning them effortlessly—worked as a correspondence clerk in Amsterdam, and later on, as a commercial representative in Petersburg, where, at the age of 27 he went into business for himself, becoming a prosperous merchant by the age of 47. Having, by then, acquired the necessary capital, a series of excavations served as the start of the realization of his childhood dream. He married a greek young lady, and settled in Athens, his interests divided between archaeology and trade (the latter served in financing the archaeological excavations he conducted). He died in Naples, on Christmas Day of 1890, during a trip he had undertaken.

Schliemann began by conducting excavations in Troy in 1871, under the influence of a romantic intention of reviving the scenery of the trojan war which Homer had described so well. Later on, he became involved with the mycenaean centres of Greece, but returned to Troy repeatedly. The most positive result of his work is that he did locate the correct site of the city on the hill of Hissarlik, and not in the region of the village of Bounarbashi, where many scholars had been searching for Troy.

He conducted an exploratory excavation at M y c e n a e , in 1874, and continued in 1876, at which time he revealed Grave Circle A, with golden funerary offerings weighing 14 kilos. In due time, while continuing his excavations in Tiryns and Orchomenos, he improved his methods of excavation and the quality of his publications which gradually lost their amateur style.

The Greek Archaeological Society supervised Schliemann's excavations through ephor Pan. Stamatakes. Following the successful excavation of 1876, the Society continued the work, with Stamatakes at first, and then with ephor Chr. Tsountas. Shortly after the First World War and until the eve of the Second (off and on, from 1921 to 1939), Alan Wace continued the excavations, as head of the British Archaeological School of Athens. The conclusions that were drawn after the pre-war excavations are to be found in summary form, along with rich bibliography, in Wace's book "Mycenae, an Archaeological History and Guide", 1949, and, following the excavations of Grave Circle B, in G. Mylonas' books, "Mycenae and the Mycenaean Age", 1966, and "Mycenae, a Guide to its Ruins and History", 1967.

The first limited excavation which was conducted in T i r y n s , was supervised by F. Thiersch, in 1831. Along with the excavation of Grave Gircle A in Mycenae, Schliemann conducted an exploratory excavation in Tiryns, and published the first report in his book "Mykenae", in 1878. He repeated the excavation in 1884 and 1885, along with the young architect W. Dörpfeld, and reported his new conclusions in his book "Tiryns", which he published along with Dörpfeld in 1886. The German

35. The hill of Deiras of Argos, the remains of the shrine of pythian Apollo, the ruins of the christian basilica, and the church of prophet Elias at the top of the hill. View from the Larissa of Argos.

36. Top left: large golden ring of Mycenae. The female figure, seated under the tree, is considered a goddess. She is holding three flowers in her uplifted right hand. A small female figure, behind the seated goddess, seems to be extending her hands towards the thick leaves of the tree. In front of the goddess, three women are approaching in reverence. The first and the third woman are carrying flowers. They all seem to be lifting their left arms in supplication. The six animal-skulls, which close this representation on the left, have been associated with the custom of preserving the skulls of sacrificed animals. The sun (a circle with rays), the moon (half-moon), the clouds, a god behind a figure-eight shield, and a double axe are depicted in the sky.

Bottom: golden ring from Tiryns. A goddess is seated to the right, holding a "rhyton" in her hands (a bird is shown behind the throne). Four "daemons", or human beings disguised as daemons, are approaching the goddess carrying cups for mixing wine. As was customary, the sun, the moon, and the stars are depicted in the sky.

Right: winged griffons on a mycenaean ring.

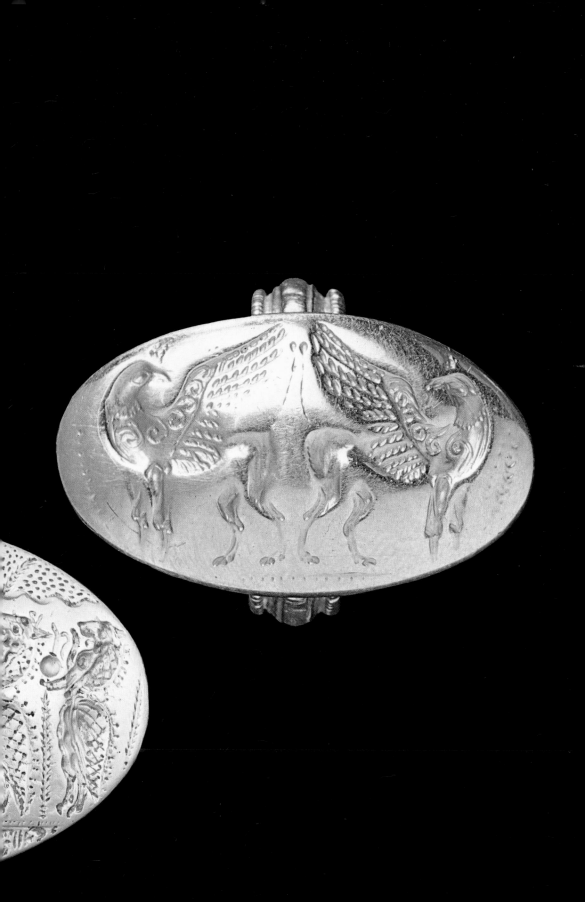

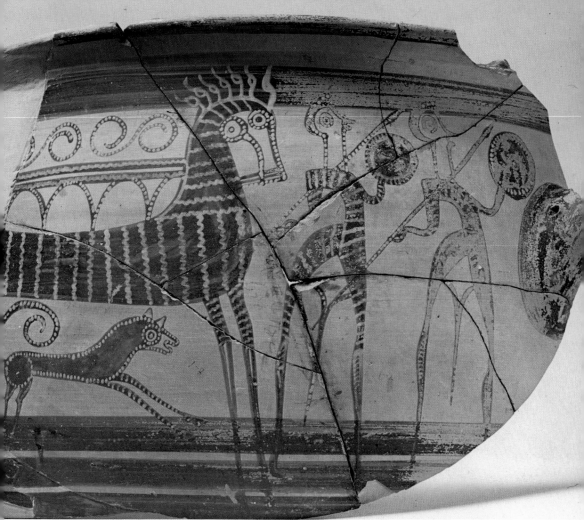

37. A fragment of a large "crater" (mixing vessel) from Tiryns. It bears representations of figures instead of the customary decorative motifs. A chariot, and two male figures, carrying a shield in the left and a spear in the right hand, are represented. The presence of a dog signifies that this is the scene of a hunt rather than one of war.

38. The acropolis of Mycenae (air-photograph). The so-called grave of Aigisthos is visible, bottom right. In the middle, the Lion Gate and Grave Circle A stand out inside the wall, along with the megaron and its court-yard above them (Reconstruction).

Archaeological Institute of Athens took over the excavations in Tiryns in 1905, and is still working on the site, having published a series of volumes; the conclusions of all the work, that has and is still being conducted, has been published under the general title, "Tiryns, die Ergebnisse der Ausgrabungen des Instituts". The first two volumes were published in 1912 and concern the shrine of Hera in Tiryns, the cemetery of the geometric period, and the wall paintings of the megaron. The third volume, published in 1930 pertains to buildings on the acropolis, and the megaron. The next five volumes (till 1975) include the conclusions drawn after the excavations conducted at the walled lower acropolis, as well as the lower city of Tiryns, along with various other sites around it. The pottery which has been excavated at different times, the tholos tomb, and all the inscriptions in Linear B which have been found in Tiryns, are all being examined.

There were no ruins in evidence at the H e r a i o n of Argos, so Schliemann showed no interest in this site. The first small-scale excavation at that site was conducted by A. R. Rangavis, along with C. Bursian, in 1854, and brought to light the first sculptured members of the 5th century temple of Hera. In the spring of 1892, Charles Waldstein, who was the head of the American School of Classical Studies of Athens, began an extensive excavation along with numerous other co-workers. He worked intensively during the spring of 1893, 1894, and 1895, employing 150-200 workmen each year, and published the conclusions of these excavations in "The Argive Heraeum", whose first volume (related to the buildings of the shrine, and its sculptured embellishment) was published in 1902, and the second (concerning smaller artifacts, statuettes of pottery, clay reliefs, potsherds, bronze objects and coins) in 1905. Mycenaean graves and other artifacts, found in the general area of the Heraeum, which belonged to prehistoric Prosymna, were published by Carl Blegen in an extensive monograph, "Prosymna, the Helladic Settlement Preceding the Argive Heraeum", 1937.

The Greek Archaeological Society, under P. Kavvadias, began its excavations at the A s k l e p i e i o n of Epidaurus in 1881. Before the excavations only the theatre was visible, with rows of benches and the cavea literary drowned within the dense growth of shrubbery, as well as the Tholos, whose circular shape was evident among the bushes. Kavvadias continued his work there for a period of over 10 years. He compiled his conclusions in the monograph "The Shrine of Asklepios in Epidaurus", which was published in 1900. Another monograph of monumental dimensions, "Épidaure, restauration et description des principaux monuments du sanctuaire d'Asclépios", had been published by H. Lechat, and A. Defrasse, in 1895, before Kavvadias' publication. Many other monographs were published later on, in connection with the theatre, the temples and the shrine of Maleatas.

The excavations of A r g o s which were conducted relatively late, were the most difficult because the contemporary city occupies the site of the ancient city. Before excavations began, segments of the ancient fortifications of Larissa were in evidence. The medieval walls had been superposed upon the ancient, which are in a good state of preservation, as well as sections of the ancient walls of the second acropolis (of Deirada). The 67 rows of benches of the theatre (many carved out of the rock) have been preserved, as well as the large brick edifice of the roman baths, which stands in front of the theatre. The nymphaeum on the eastern slope of Larissa, as well as a section of the reservoir were also known. Systematic excavations began in the early years of the century, with reports originally published in the Bulletin de Correspondence Héllénique, 1904, and then sporadically until 1930. Following the war, the French School of Archaeology resumed excavations and its reports have been published uninterrupted, since 1952. Along with these publications, the French School has published quite a few monographs with partial conclusions of these excavations, or phase of work; W. Vollgraff, "Le sanctuaire d'Apollon Pythéen à Argos", 1956, and G. Roux, "L'architecture de l'Argolide aux siècles 4. et 3. av. J.C.", 1961 (with a reconsideration of Vollgraff's views concerning the sanctuary of the pythian Apollo in Deiras). J. Deshayes, "Les fouilles de la Deiras", 1966, (concerning mycenaean graves), and René Ginouvés, "Le théâtron à gradins droits et l'Odéon d'Argos", 1972, (concerning the odeum and the older theatre, with straight rows of benches, which was located in Argos) have also published their reports.

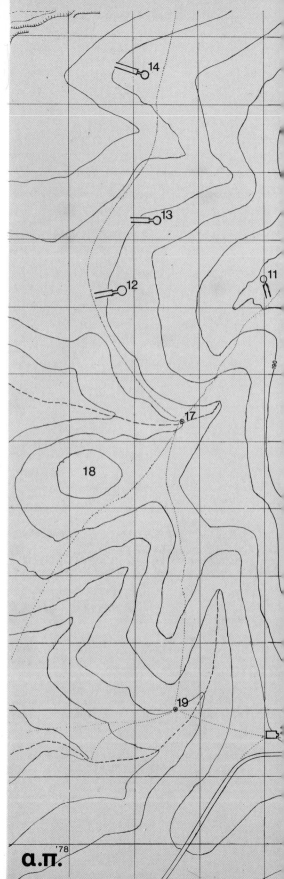

39. Topographical ground plan of Mycenae and the surrounding country-side. **1.** Scant remains of a mycenaean structure; it is located on the road between Mycenae and the Heraeum, or between Mycenae and Argos, a road which crosses a spring of water at this point. **2.** Remains of a rural shrine, where Agamemnon was worshipped during the historical period. A shrine of greater renown, dedicated to the same god, existed at Amykles, in Lakonia. Originally, this was a god of the underworld. However, during the historical period, and under the influence of epic poetry, many identified this god with Agamemnon, the king of Mycenae. **3.** The Treasury of Atreus (see p. 62). **4.** Traces of the time when Mycenae, constituted a "kome" of Argos during the post-classical period. **5.** Scant ruins of the mycenaean period. **5A.** The so-called "Oil-Merchant's" house (p. 63), in the middle of a complex of mycenaean structures. **6.** The tomb of Clytemestra (p. 63). **7.** The "so-called" royal Grave Circle B (p. 68). **8.** Scant remains of statuettes in the cavea of the small hellenistic theatre in Mycenae (p. 68). **9.** The "so-called" tholos tomb of Aigisthos (p. 68). **10.** The so-called tholos tomb of the "lions" (this tomb has been named after its location in the immediate vicinity of the Lion Gate (p. 68). **11.** A tholos tomb, known as "pano fournou" (upper oven); one of the oldest of its kind. **12.** A tholos tomb, called "cyclopeian". It has most of the characteristics of the most ancient graves of its kind (p. 68). **13.** A tholos tomb, named ' the Daemons", after the glass tiles which were found in it, and which represent "Daemons" (imaginary beings carrying cups for mixing wine). It has not been dated among the oldest tombs. **14.** A tholos tomb, known as that of "kato fournou" (lower oven). **15.** A tholos tomb, named "Tes Panagias" (after the small church of "Our Virgin" which is located higher up). **16.** The church of "Our Virgin". **17.** The upper well. **18.** The hill of Kalkani. **19.** The lower well. **20.** The small church of Agh. Georgios. **21.** The torrent, Chavos. (Plan by Dr. Argyres Petronotes, based on an older one from the Doxiades' Athens Centre of Ekistics).

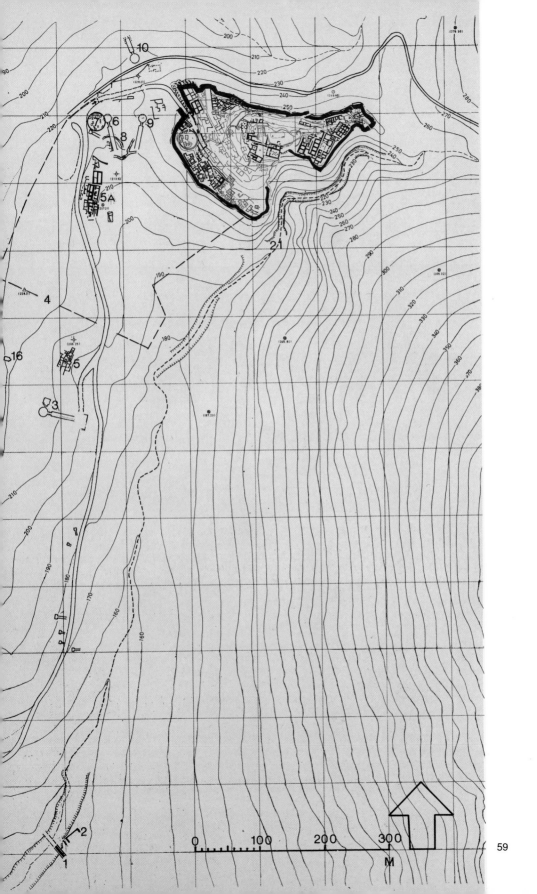

59

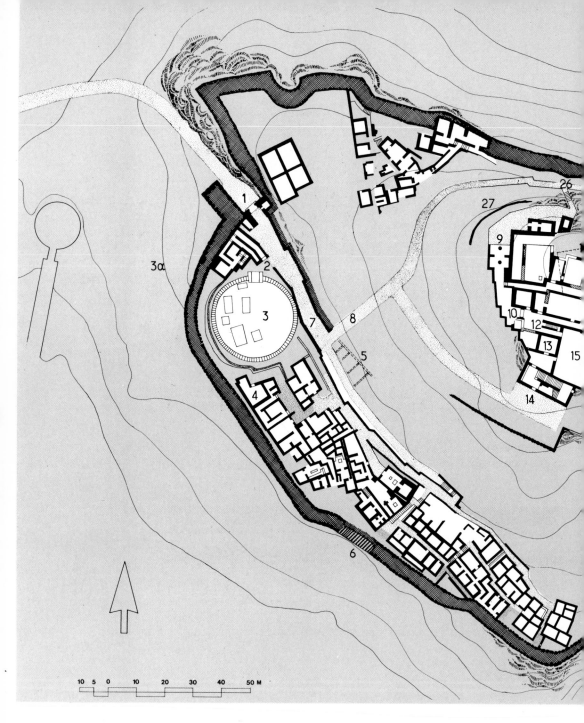

40. The acropolis of Mycenae. The foundations of the prehistoric buildings have been drawn with a thick black line. The other foundations belong to buildings of the town of the historical period. 1. The Lion Gate. 2. A building attached to the fortified enclosure ("granary"). 3. Royal Grave Circle A. 3a. Prehistoric grave-yard (a continuation of the one inside the walls). 4. The house where the "crater" (mixing bowl or cup) with the warrior-representation was found. 5. Hellenistic building (oil-press). 6. A section of the polygonal wall (a hellenistic repair). 7. Uphill ramp to the megaron. 8. The road to the top of the hill and the megaron. 9. Propylon in the area of the palace. 10. The threshold of the entrance to the corridor 11 (it exists at its original position). 11. Passage to the north of the megaron. 12. Passage to the court of the palace. 13.

40

*Guest-room. **14.** Monumental staircase (leading to the one towards the guest-room, or the court-yard of the palace). **15.** The court-yard of the megaron. **16.** The megaron. **17.** Private quarters of the sovereign (at a higher level). **18.** Hellenistic temple of Hera (or Athena). **19.** Work-shops. **20.** Large house with a central peristyle court-yard. **21.** Descent to the secret subterranean cistern. **22.** Gallery (narrow passage towards the north). **23.** Gallery towards the south. **24.** Circular hellenistic cistern. **25.** Northern gate of the prehistoric wall. **26.** Staircase. **27.** Scant (hypothetical) traces of an older fortification enclosure (middle-helladic) which surrounded the higher part of the hill only.*
(Plan, by E. Moutopoulos, based on a recent one by G. Mylonas).

2. Mycenae

A. Outside the Acropolis

From the village of Phichtia, which is located on the main road between Corinth and Argos, at a distance of approximately 8 kilometres outside Argos, an asphalt road runs through the contemporary village of Mycenae (former Charvati), and then leads uphill towards ancient Mycenae. To the left of this road, the openings of small chamber tombs (a few of the many that have been excavated in this area) are quite visible. The rock, or c h a m b e r tombs, which are carved out of the stony slopes, usually consist of one "four-sided chamber," or upon rare occasions, a circular one, which could be approached through a "dromos" (in other words, a ditch which sloped downward towards the opening of the chamber). These were family graves, as was the case even of the tholos tombs. The dead were laid on the ground of the chamber, one beside the other, the funerary offerings placed on the ground, as well. Upon rare occasions, pits were dug into the ground and the dead were buried in these.

Of the nine t h o l o s tombs which are known in Mycenae, the seven are located in the hills to the left of the road, at a shorter or longer distance from it (see pl. on p. 59). Only two have been located to the right, the so-called tombs of Clytemestra and Aigisthos, which were built in the area of the "middle helladic cemetery", in the immediate vicinity of the Lion Gate.

The so-called T r e a s u r y o f A t r e u s (number **3**, on the plan on p. 59), is located closer to the road (to the left, as one ascends towards the acropolis). It is the largest and most impressive of all the tombs that have been discovered in Mycenae. Its "dromos" is 36 metres long, 6 metres wide, and its side walls are lined with large solid ashlar breccia masonry, fitted in horizontal courses. Its doorway, "stomion", measures 5,40 metres high, 2,66 metres wide, at the lower, and 2,46 metres at the upper level. A double door used to close the opening, this being quite evident from the pivot-holes on the threshold and lintels. The façade of the entrance was framed on either side, by engaged columns of green alabaster, each with sculptured decorations on the surface. Similar relief-decorations had been carved on the stone slab which covered the triangular relieving opening. The lintel consisted of two blocks of stone, the innermost of the two being the largest, with a length of 8 metres, a width of 5 and breadth of 1,20 metres. Its weight has been calculated at 120,000 kilos. This block had been pulled up a dirt ramp which was then cleared away, after the stone had been placed in position. It had, then, been carved to follow the concave inner surface of the tholos (see below). The "Treasury of Atreus" has a diameter of 14,5 metres, and a height of 13,2 metres. The tholos had been constructed in the corbelled manner, with dressed ashlar blocks, in 34 horizontal courses (the dome is not constructed on the vault principle; the courses simply project one over another, uncemented, by decreasing the diameter of the concentric circles. The top was covered by a single stone, hollowed on the underside to continue the curve of the tholos. This stone is the "key" of the tholos. The embedded bronze pins apparently fastened rosettes of bronze, or other decorative motifs of the interior surface of the tholos. A smaller irregular four-sided chamber adjoins the tholos on its northern part. Its opening is 2,5 metres high and 1,5 metres wide. The triangular relieving opening above the lintel, as well as the pivot holes on the threshold, prove the existence of a double door. The remaining tholos tombs of Mycenae do not have this adjoining chamber. The imposing "Treasury of Minyas" at Orchomenos has such a chamber, as well as other smaller tholos tombs in other parts of Greece. The "Treasury of Atreus" has been dated at

1330 B.C. (Wace). The view that it might be dated a century later, has been expressed lately, and so the date of its construction would coincide with the date during which the mythical king Atreus is supposed to have lived. This date (circa 1250 B.C.) has been accepted for the monumental walls of the acropolis, which include the Lion Gate, as well (G. Mylonas).

As one approaches closer to the acropolis, one comes across, (on the right side) the foundations of the private mycenaean homes; one of these is called the House of the Oil Merchant because large pithoi were found in an oil storage room (number **5A** on plan p. 59). A good number of clay tablets inscribed with Linear B were also found in this house. A similar tablet was found to the north of this house, in another one which consisted of two oblong rooms.

To the right of the road, higher up the hill, one reaches the so-called "Tomb of Clytemestra" (number **6** on the plan p. 59), which is considered as the most recent of all the tholos tombs (circa 1220 B.C.). The walls of the "dromos" (37 metres long and 6 metres wide) were also dressed with ashlar conglomerate masonry. The

41. Present view of the acropolis of Mycenae.

42. The Lion gate; the voluminous stone lintel with the relieving lion triangle.

43. The Lion gate of Mycenae between two high branches of the wall.

44. The acropolis of Mycenae; the Lion gate, viewed from the interior.

45. The "Treasury of Atreus" in Mycenae; the "dromos" and the "entrance".

46. The entrance façade of the "Treasury of Atreus". (Reconstruction).

47. The "Treasury of Atreus". View of the interior of the tholos facing the entrance. The large stone lintel follows the curve of the tholos.

48. The acropolis of Mycenae; ascent towards the top of the hill, where the palace is located.

45

façade of the opening presents decorations similar to those of the "Treasury of Atreus" on the engaged columns.

Grave circle B (number **7** on the plan) was discovered during the work on the restoration of this tomb. The enclosure had been built with a diameter of 27 metres, and only a small section in a good state of preservation. Part of this enclosure had been destroyed by the Mycenaeans themselves, during prehistoric times, in order to accommodate Clytemestra's tomb. Twenty five shaft graves (some of them rather large family graves) had been dug into this enclosure. Some of these are older than those of Grave Circle A, while others are contemporary to them. An abundance of grave offerings, of the middle-helladic period, was found, along with bronze swords, vessels of rock-crystal, necklaces, and a large quantity of gold-leaf jewelry, as was the case with the graves of Grave Circle A, inside the acropolis.

A small theatre (number **8** on plan p. 59), whose cavea cut across part of the dromos, was built in front of the tomb of Clytemestra by the Mycenaeans of the hellenistic town.

Another tholos tomb, closer to the Lion Gate (between this and Clytemestra's tomb), has been called the tomb of Aigisthos (number **9**, on plan p. 59). This is older than Clytemestra's grave by more than two and a half centuries; its façade was decorated with an ashlar porous wall when it was re-used at a later date, during the mycenaean period.

Another tomb, located opposite and at a short distance from the Lion Gate, known as "the tholos Lion tomb" is also more than a century and a half older than Clytemestra's tomb. Wace paid close attention to the dating of the tholos tombs, which he based on the special features and characteristics of each one. According to these, the tholos tombs can be placed in three categories. The most recent of all are those of the Atreus and Clytemestra type, whose "dromoi" are carefully dressed with ashlar masonry; the façades of the openings are also covered with the same type of masonry and are decorated with engaged columns. The surfaces of these columns, as well as the slabs which cover the triangular relief openings, bear sculptured decorations. Their openings were closed with heavy wooden doors which were covered with bronze. Those tholos tombs, which were somewhat older, consisted of carelessly dressed "dromos" walls and second-rate decorations on the façade of the opening. Finally, the oldest of all had an unlined dromos; their openings were not closed by doors, but were shut up with stone walls; large blocks, whose surface had not been dressed carefully, were used as jambs; the blocks which were used as lintels were not carved on the inside to follow the concave curve of the tholos. Last of all, the tholos, itself, was built with rubble, and had no relieving triangle over the lintel of the opening.

B. Inside the Acropolis

The acropolis of Mycenae had two large entrances, one on the western side (the Lion Gate), which was the main and most impressive one, and another to the north. The plan of both is similar; the lion gate is located at the deep recess of a narrow passage which is created by two branches of the wall. The height of these two branches, which had been re-enforced by towers, made it possible for the defenders of the acropolis to repel any attack aimed at forcing the gates.

The open area in front of the Lion Gate (number **1** on plan p. 60) was 15 metres long and had a width of about half its length. The gate itself is made up of four blocks of stone; the threshold, 4,65 metres long, 2,31 metres wide and approx. 88 centimetres thick; the lintel is more than 4,5 metres long, and approximately 2 metres wide, with two pilasters (to the right and left) 3,10 metres high, and 1,74

49. The palace of Mycenae. The sole remains of a building that were revealed during excavations. Below, the monumental stone-staircase which led to the court-yard of the megaron. The south-east corner of the megaron had collapsed in the ravine below—it has since been restored. Remains of a guest-room to the west of the court-yard. (Plan by Wace).

50. The palace of Mycenae; the court-yard of the megaron. The megaron is visible in the background.

51. The acropolis of Mycenae; the northern gate of the fortification wall.

52. Top left: one of the golden masks of Grave Circle A in Mycenae, the one called ''Agamemnon's'' (16th century B.C.). Right: two other golden masks from the kings' graves of the same Circle A.

49

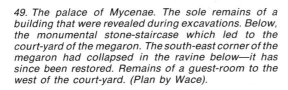

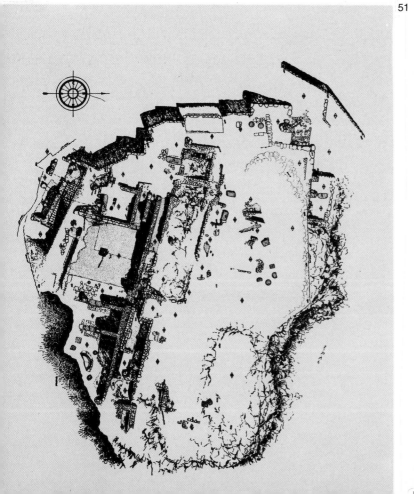

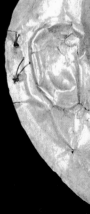

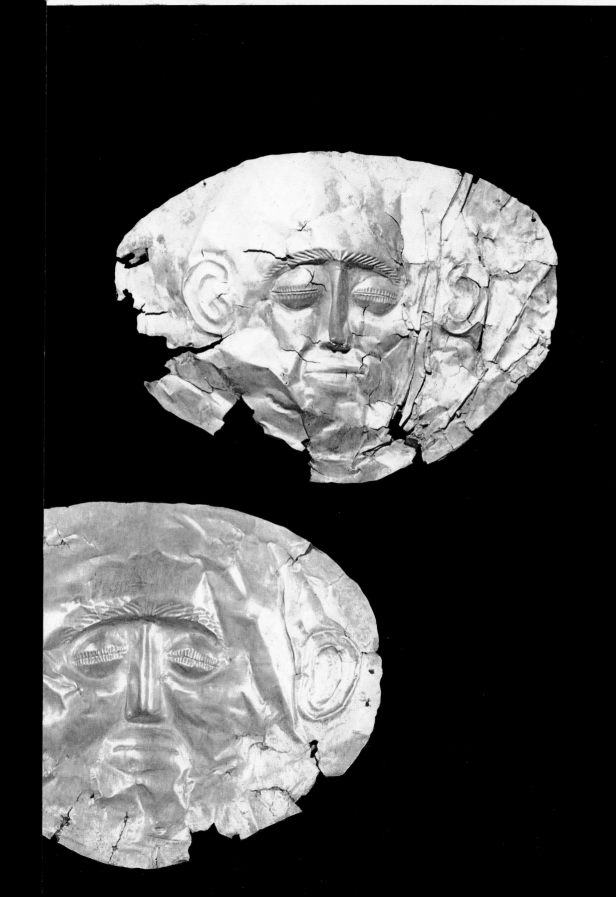

metres wide. The opening between the 4 blocks of stone is as high as the pilasters (3,10 metres), and is about 3 metres wide (the width is somewhat less at a higher level). A wooden double door, which was covered with bronze, closed the opening (the pivot-holes are visible on the lintel). On the inside, the gate could be closed with a cross-bar (the holes which held this cross-bar are visible on the pilasters). The sculpture of the lions (lionesses) on the relieving triangle is 3,30 metres high, and 3,90 metres wide at the lower level. The view that these animals represented griffons (their heads are quite worn out) is not supported by Pausanias' description, who irrefutably calls them "lions" (2,16,5), while, in other sections of his work, he not only describes sculptures, or paintings of griffons, but determines the form of these imaginary beings with great accuracy (1,25,6).

The section of the walls, with the gate and the massive tower on the right, has been considered an addition to an earlier fortified enclosure. The old fortification has been dated in the middle of the 14th century B.C. It seems to have been restored in the middle of the 13th century, when the impressive gate was built for the first time, and Grave Circle A, which had been located outside the wall, was enclosed within the new fortification walls. The section of the wall, which, as a result, formed a curve for the sake of the graves, cut into the middle of the great cemetery that was located on the site, and which extended at least to Grave Circle B, and the area near the tomb of Clytemestra.

Upon passing through the gate, one sees, to the right, an edifice which rests on the fortified enclosure of the acropolis, which is used as one of its walls (number **2**

53

53. Restoration of the northwest corner of the court-yard in the palace of Mycenae. A second storey had been built over the so-called guest-room, a fact which makes the possibility of another storey on all sides quite tenable, and more so on the side opposite the megaron.

54. The "dromos" and the entrance of the so-called "Tomb of Clytemestra."

on the plan). This building, which had two storeys, was probably used by the guards at the gate, who were responsible for its opening and shutting during times of peace; it is known as the g r a n a r y, due to the pithoi with grains of wheat which were found at ground level.

G r a v e c i r c l e A (number **3**) was excavated in front of the "granary". This circle has a diameter of approximately 28 metres, and is formed by a circular double row of upright slabs. Six unlooted family graves (rectangular shaft graves), where 19 dead had been buried altogether (nine men, eight women, and two children), were revealed inside this grave circle. The smallest grave has the following dimensions: 3,05 × 2,15 metres, and the largest 6,55 × 4,10 metres. Bronze swords, gold masks, diadems, and hundreds of decorated leaves of gold (the total weight of golden objects is approximately 14 kilos), along with numerous other artifacts were found in these graves. The burials and funerary offerings are dated in the 16th century B.C., but the enclosure with the upright slabs is supposed to have been built in later years. The upright slabs bore carved reliefs of men in war chariots, or other simpler decorative themes.

P r i v a t e h o u s e s, built quite close together, were excavated to the south of the grave circle. Many remains of the town buildings of the historical period were revealed, as well (see plan p. 60 and accompanying legend).

An u p w a r d r a m p (number **7**) led to the top of the hill, where the palace was

55. Grave Circle A (inside the Lion gate) along with the uphill ramp to the top of the acropolis of Mycenae.

located during mycenaean times. This wide ramp became narrower as it progressed upward, and ended at the p r o p y l o n (number **9**), with a stoa in front and back, and one column in antis both in front and back, which served as supports of the roof. Upon passing the propylon, one approached towards the long narrow passage **11**, which had a door at point **10,** whose threshold is still in situ. One could approach the great c o u r t o f t h e p a l a c e (number **15**), through passage **11**. It could also be reached from a second passage (number **12**) which ran parallel to the first. Room **13** (dimensions 6,2 × 5,5 metres) seems to have been a g u e s t - r o o m. This room had a vestibule in front which was accessible by a staircase leading to a third passage, located between passages **11** and **12,** one that was narrower than the other two.

One could approach the palace and the guest-room from the south, where the m o n u m e n t a l s t a i r c a s e **14** was located at a lower level. The entire lower section of the masonry of a staircase has been preserved, along with the landing, at which point the two upper sections started, after a turn of 180 degrees. This section ended at the vestibule of the guest-room which was located on the same level as the great palace court. Since the guest-room and its vestibule had an upper storey, it is only natural to assume that the palace façade had two storeys, at least over the stoa of the façade and the vestibule. If that were not the case, the megaron would have given the impression of a structure by far less elegant than the guest-room. The area (number **16**) inside consisted of the main megaron, with four central columns supporting the roof, which had an opening in the middle through which smoke could escape, and a circular hearth in the middle of the floor. The megaron was probably only one storey high, although there is a probability that it had two storeys, with a second opening on the roof of the vestibule which had been constructed on the same axis as the former one. The walls of the main megaron and the vestibule had been decorated with wall paintings (a few small pieces, where men, horses and chariots were depicted, have been found). The main megaron (the area with the hearth) is approximately 11,5 metres wide, and 13 metres long. The diameter of the hearth is 3,40 metres. The southeastern corner of the megaron, along with the base of the column, which was located on the same spot, have collapsed in the ravine

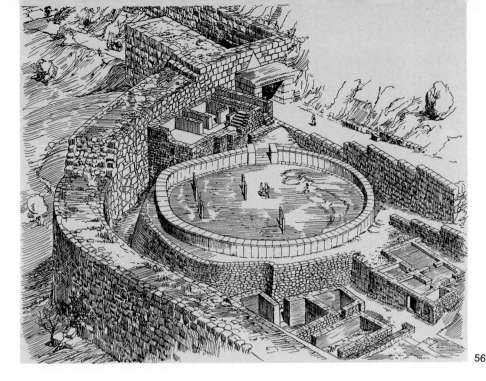

56. Reconstruction of Grave Circle A (Wace). Because of the enclosure, the wall of the acropolis bears a curved configuration. Stone "stelae" were placed over the shaft graves.

below, along with a section of the fortification wall. These sections were restored recently.

To the north of the megaron, at a higher level, small sections of the walls of the various rooms have been preserved. These probably belong to the ruler's apartments. It seems that the greater part of these apartments disappeared, following a levelling of the hill-top which took place in the geometric period, before the erection of a t e m p l e on that spot. The first temple was small; inadequate traces having been preserved only. This was not dedicated to Athena, but rather to Hera, along with the neighbouring large shrine at the foot of Mount Euboea, known as the Heraeum of Argos which originally used to be the main shrine of Mycenae, as well. During the late historical period, a larger temple was rebuilt on the acropolis of Mycenae, which had a very unusual orientation, from north to south. A section only of this more recent temple, the "krepidoma" (the stepped platform of a Greek temple) has been preserved in situ (number **18** on the plan).

Numerous building remains have been revealed in the area to the east of the megaron. It seems that the most significant belong to a house with many rooms, and a central peristyle court (number **20** on the plan).

Until the second half of the late-helladic III period, the eastern extremity of the fortified enclosure was located somewhat to the east of the building, at the site of the subterranean water cistern, which was accessible by a staircase. Shortly before 1200 B.C., the enclosure was extended to the east and took in the opening of the staircase to the cistern (number **21** on the plan), in a manner that the besieged mycenaeans could descend unimpeded to the water cistern which was located outside the wall, deep under the surface of the ground. The staircase of the approach has been preserved, and today, one is able to reach the dark bottom of the cistern.

The second gate of the fortification wall (known as the "north gate"), which was similar to the Lion Gate but of a smaller scale, is 2,30 metres high, and 1,40 metres wide at the lower level, and lies a short distance to the west of the secret cistern.

58

57. The handles of mycenaean swords, with linings of decorated golden plates.

58. A mycenaean vessel bearing the reproduction of a row of soldiers on march (to the left, a woman is bidding them farewell).

59. A mycenaean vessel of steatite (15th century B.C.). Carved decorations with polypods. The vessel is a pyxis with a punctured bottom. The upper part (the shoulders of the vessel) constitute the tap with the handle at the top. The interior diameter of the cavity is 13 centimetres. The liquid which was poured in this vessel was then drained through the ten holes in the bottom.

60. Carved ivory representation; two female figures and a child (from Mycenae).

61. Gold ornament from the shaft gravès in Mycenae; a representative example of mycenaean miniature workmanship.

62. Golden diadem from the graves in Grave Circle A in Mycenae, (1550 B.C.). Gold plates with rich decorations in relief.

63. Another gold diadem with richer decorations.

64

65

64. *Lime head of a female figure
from the excavations in Mycenae.
The lips, the eyes, the hair, as well
as the ornaments on the face have
been rendered in colour.*

65. *Decoration on the blade of a
mycenaean knife; a lion-hunt with
a group of hunters.*

66. *Clay statuette from Mycenae,
presently in the museum of Nauplion (13th century B.C.). The two
necklaces, two bracelets, the fa-
cial details, and the ornaments on
the dress have been rendered in
colour.*

3. The Heraeum of Argos

A road from the contemporary village of Mycenae (Charvati) to the Heraeum passes through the village of Monasteraki. From the Heraeum, this same road descends towards Chonika. Today, it is best to follow the paved road from Heraeum - Chonica - Argos. The remains of the famous shrine are located on the slope of a hill at the foot of Mount Euboea. It has been assumed that the acropolis of the prehistoric city of "Prosymna" was located at the top of this low hill. During the mycenaean period, Prosymna was the closest city to Mycenae. It would seem that close political and social bonds existed between the two cities. Prosymna was a settlement, dependent on Mycenae, and connected with it by a road 5 kilometres long. Traces of this road, as well as bridges over ravines are still extant today. During the mycenaean period monumental fortifications, to be used for the defense of both in case of external danger, had been built only on Mycenae. The number of chamber tombs that have been excavated over a large area, to the northwest of the Heraeum (towards the direction of Mycenae), prove the prosperity and growth of Prosymna during the early mycenaean era. The neolithic settlement on that site was probably quite flourishing, even more so than Mycenae. Tools and neolithic potsherds have been found, not only at the site of the Heraeum, but to the west of this area, as well, at sites that were quite distant from each other.

Following the mycenaean period, both Prosymna and Mycenae survived as insignificant towns. Shortly after the persian wars, the Argives destroyed both settlements simultaneously. Before the dispute, which led to the destruction of those towns, the Argives had already appropriated the cult of prosymnaia Hera. During the archaic period, the Heraeum was considered the principal argive shrine. The Argives not only built the most famous 5th century temple with the chryselephantine (gold and ivory) statue of Hera, but the old temple of the goddess, as well, along with stoas, and other edifices connected to the temple. A road, 8 kilometres long, had been constructed at that time, and led from Argos to the shrine. After the construction of this new road, the old one from Mycenae to the Heraeum was not used anymore, as has happened today with the road from Argos - Chonica - Heraeum.

The exact nature of the cult of Hera is not clear. Of all the available archaeological sources and data, the story of Kleobis and Viton, as Herodotus (1,31) wrote it, seems the most feasible: the mother of these two young men, who was a priestess of Hera, prayed to the goddess that her sons "be given the best fate that a man may receive". The goddess, then, granted death to Kleobis and Viton, during the night that they spent sleeping in her temple. This can be interpreted as follows: Hera's cult was associated with secret teachings which had the purpose of familiarizing the initiates with death. The initiation, which most probably was originally conducted in the inner sanctuary, later on took place within a special columned hall which resembled somewhat the "telesterion" (a hall of ceremonies used as a hall of "mysteries") in Eleusis. This hall was restored at the end of the 5th century, at the time of the building of the new temple of Hera, and was in use throughout the entire period of antiquity. The mystic teachings which had been enriched (probably under the influence of the eleusinian mysteries) gave Hera, not only the attributes of a goddess of the underworld, but those of a goddess of fertility of fauna, flora, and of human beings. This role was associated with all the chthonian gods, and marked the characteristics of the Achaian cults which were later on accepted by the Dorians, and flourished during historical times.

The cult of the goddess had originated in the region of the Heraeum, where, sometime close to 680 B.C., the so-called "old temple" of Hera had been constructed (number **13**, plan p. 88-89), on an area which had already been levelled in the past. A smaller cult edifice, or a sacred open enclosure, with an altar, had probably been constructed before the building of the "old temple". The wall, which

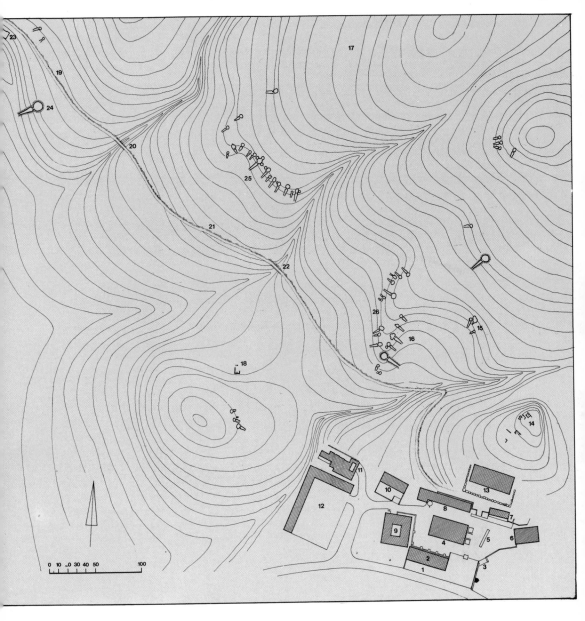

67. Topographical diagram of the region of ancient Prosymna and the Heraeum of Argos. **1-13.** The sanctuary of Hera. **14.** Installations of mycenaean and older periods (of prehistoric Prosymna). **15, 16,** and **17.** Locations of neolithic finds. **18.** A mycenaean house. **19, 20,** and **21.** Ancient road between Mycenae and the Heraeum. **22.** Remains of a prehistoric bridge spanning a small ravine. **23.** Probable ancient shrine. **24.** Mycenaean tholos tomb. **25, 26.** Main cemeteries of Prosymna, with tholos tombs.
(Plan by A. Moutopoulou, based on a previous one by C. Blegen).

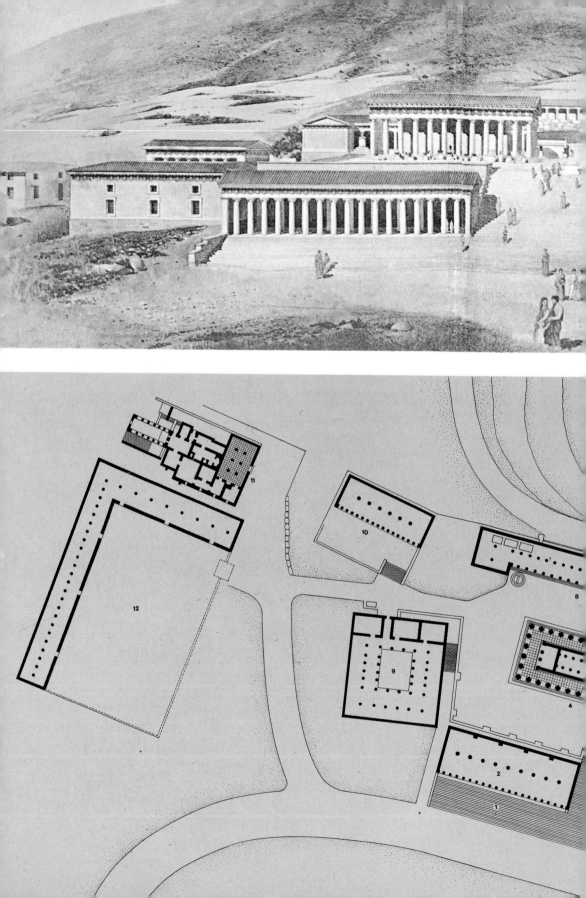

68

68. *Restoration of the Heraeum of Argos (Waldstein).*

69. *The Heraeum of Argos. The foundations of buildings which were revealed during excavations.*
1. *Monumental escalated retaining wall.* **2.** *Stoa on the levelled western section of the retaining wall.* **3.** *Small eastern staircase leading to the level area of the temple.*
4. *New temple of Hera.*
5. *Altar, to the east of the temple.* **6.** *A rectangular structure (the so-called "telesterion") with rows of columns supporting its roof.* **7** *and* **8.** *Stoas to the north of the new temple. A staircase, located between the two stoas, led to the levelled area of the old temple.* **9.** *Large rectangular building with an interior peristyle and an open court-yard in the middle. The edifice was used for symposia.*
10. *Western stoa with a levelled area along the façade.* **11.** *Roman "thermai" (baths).*
12. *Gymnasium, or guest-house.* **13.** *Old temple of Hera.*
(Plan by A. Moutopoulou, based on a previous one by Waldstein).

69

had been constructed to the south of the temple in order to hold in place the soil of the embankment, has been dated, no later than the 8th century B.C. According to what we can assume from those parts of its foundations which are extant, this temple has all the characteristics of the early greek temples, especially those with the elongated cella (36,5×8,5 metres). The dimensions of the krepidoma were 47 × 18,75 metres. The inner sanctuary was surrounded by a pteron (the wing or flank colonnade of a temple) of 6×14 wooden columns. The roof of the temple was wooden, as well as most parts of the entablature. As a result, the building was easy prey to the fire that destroyed it in 423 B.C. The Argives did not restore this temple, but built the new one on the next level which was lower, having been levelled in the past for the annual festival in honour of the goddess. An altar was located on that site, and it is known that sacrifices of many bulls (hekatombes), and public feasts

used to take place during the festivities. Since the old temple was highly revered by the people of Argolis, the Argives did not discard its ruins, but left them untouched, building an enclosure around them. Pausanias viewed these remains in situ, approximately 580 years later.

The new temple, which was built according to the plans of the Argive architect Eupolemos, was completed shortly after 410 B.C. It was a stone edifice on a krepidoma - 39,65 × 20,10 metres - and a peristyle of 6 × 12 columns. The cella had a "pronaos" (a porch before the main temple or cella), and a porch in the back, with two columns each, at both façades. In the interior, a colonnade of 5 doric superposed columns had been raised to the right and left. A second colonnade, of an equal number of doric columns, which supported the roof, had also been constructed above the lower colonnade. The chryselephantine cult statue of the

70

70. The "krepidoma"
(stepped platform of a
greek temple) of the "new"
temple of Hera, at the
Heraeum of Argos. View
from the site of the "old"
temple of the goddess
which is located at a higher
level.

71. A "stoa" of the
Heraeum of Argos (number
2 on plan 69).

72. The embankment of the
"old" temple of Hera at the
Heraeum of Argos
(a somewhat careless
construction, of stone
blocks, is visible at the top).

goddess had been placed in a deep recess of the cella, and depicted the goddess sitting on a throne, holding a sceptre in her left, and a pomegranate in her right hand. During the hellenistic and roman periods, tradition had it that the statue was the work of the famous 5th-century Argive sculptor Polykleitos. The chryselephantine statue of the goddess Hebe had been placed opposite the statue of Hera. According to tradition, again, this statue was the work of the sculptor Naukydes, the brother, or nephew of Polykleitos. A small wooden statue of Hera, which the Argives had brought from Tiryns, when they destroyed the city after the persian wars was also kept in the cella. In spite of the fact that this small statue was an artless wooden image of the goddess, it was considered one of the most revered sacred objects by the Argives. It depicted the goddess seated, as in the case of Polykleitos' chryselephantine statue, and tradition had it that this statue had been carved out of a piece of the trunk of a wild pear tree.

The temple was accessible by an inclined ramp whose foundations have been preserved on the east side of the krepidoma. Among other votive offerings, the marble statues of Hera's priestesses had been placed in front of the temple. The priestesses served the goddess for life, and their name, as well as the year of their priesthood constituted the local dating system of the Argives. This was customary among all the Greeks, who had similar dating systems, such as the athenian (using the "first Archon" of each year), and the spartan (with the "Spartan Ephor"). As a result, Thucydides (2,2) gives the year of the beginning of the peloponnesian war as the 48th year of the priesthood of Chrysis, which was 431 B.C. All the precious silver and gold objects, as well as those with precious stones (votive offerings of the emperors Nero and Hadrian) were kept in the temple.

A monumental escalated retaining wall (81 metres long) which served as a staircase, as well (number **1** on plan p. 88), had been built on the south side of the shrine, in order to buttress the level area upon which the 5th century temple had been built. A stoa (arcade) (number **2**) had been erected at the west end of the levelled area. This was not open to the terraced area of the temple, which was on a higher level, but to the road which led to the shrine, and ran along a lower level, at the base of the embankment. The stoa had one colonnade along the front, and a second one all along the interior. This stoa was accessible from the western end of the escalated retaining wall, while one could climb on the temple enclosure from the east, by using a small staircase with eight steps (number **3**), which was located next to the enclosure.

On the northern side, the central area used to close off with two other stoas which faced the temple (numbers **7** and **8**). These stoas were similar to the first, with two colonnades, as well, one along the façade, and the other along the middle. The eastern stoa was the smallest, with dimensions of 22 × 7,5 metres. It was located on the upper level of another similar escalated embankment. The stoa to the west was 63 metres long and 10,5 metres wide. When this area was excavated, part of the western stoa curved towards the south, presenting a ground plan in the form of a Γ. The foundations of an older structure, with a different orientation, were revealed under the foundations of the western side of the stoa. Pedestals which held votive offerings have been preserved along the façade. Three large rectangular cisterns were revealed near the northwestern corner, between the inner colonnade, and the north wall of the same stoa.

To the east, the central area of the shrine closed off with the "telesterion" (number **6**), a rectangular hall which was approximately 29 metres long and 17 metres wide. Three rows of 5 columns each were located in the interior, and three columns supported a porch, facing the large temple.

A large square building, which was located to the west of the temple (number **9** on the plan), had an interior peristyle court with arcades along the east, south and west sides, and a number of rooms along the north side. Pieces of stone tables and couches, which were found in this building, leave no doubt that it had been used for symposia.

Ruins of bathing facilities have been preserved at the northwest corner of the shrine (number **11** on the plan). These are parts of thermai (bathing establishments) with hot-air spaces under the sweating rooms (hypocausts). Areas with mosaic floors, characteristic of many roman baths had also been erected close to the shrine. These baths acquired an additional usefulness, when the festival of the Heraia was enriched with games. Some scholars believe that the large Γ - shaped structure to the south, which had probably been used as a gymnasium, or a guest-house (number **12**), must have been associated with the games of the Heraia. Its court is 74 metres long and 33,5 metres wide.

73. The most charming head of the goddess; from the Heraeum of Argos. Waldstein attributed this head to the cult statue of Hera. It may belong to a smaller statue of the goddess (not the more recent one, however, of the end of the 5th century), or to a statue of Hebe.

73

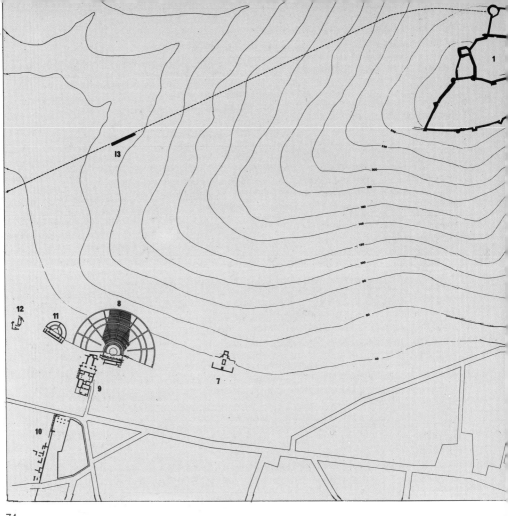

74

4. Argos

The centre of the ancient city, with the most important public buildings and temples, was located at the site of the contemporary city, making excavations extremely difficult. It is certain that the agora of Argos, with the sanctuary of lykeian Apollo, and numerous famous votive works of art, was not too far from the large theatre which was located to the east. The Argives used to place decrees (measures passed by a general assembly) in the enclosure of lykeian Apollo. A number of these has been discovered, with a specific statement engraved on the stone, stating that the decrees were to be placed in the sanctuary of this god.

The only ancient structures excavated that have been studied are located at the western end of the contemporary town, in other words, at the eastern foot of Larissa. These are a roman nymphaion, a large theatre, with a good number of benches carved on the natural rock, the imposing roman baths in front of the theatre, the odeum of Argos, and the sanctuary of Aphrodite.

The n y m p h a i o n, at a distance of 100-120 metres to the north of the theatre, consists of two rectangular cisterns, on two different levels, which used to be fed with drinking water through pipes whose traces are still in evidence to the north, on the slopes of Larissa. The outlets of the lower cistern fed with water the city of Argos, and especially the area of the neighbouring agora. The building acquired its final form during the imperial era, shortly after the birth of Christ. A level area, 35 metres long and approximately 21 metres wide, may be seen in front of the nympaion, as

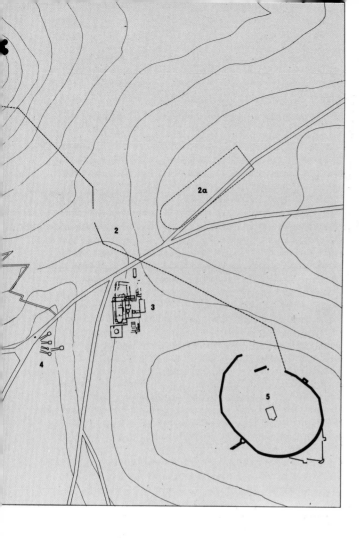

74. Topographical plan of Argos. **1.** The acropolis of Larissa. **2.** "Deiras" of Argos (defile between the two hills). **2a.** Conjectured location of the stadium. **3.** The shrine of pythian Apollo (or "deiradiotes"). **4.** Mycenaean burial grounds on Deiras. **5.** Fortified hill which constituted the second acropolis of Argos (with the church of prophet Elias at the top). **6.** Contemporary church of "Our Virgin of the Rock" (the site of the ancient shrine of Hera). **7.** The roman nymphaion and the site of the "kriterion" (an area reserved for court-hearings) of Argos. **8.** The theatre of Argos. **9.** Roman "thermai; (baths). **10.** Public edifices of the agora of Argos. **11.** The Odeum. **12.** The shrine of Aphrodite. **13.** Sections of the fortification walls. (Plan by A. Moutopoulou, based on a previous one, of the French School of Archaeology).

well as the traces of the enclosure of a pre-classical shrine. The retaining wall of this area, which is located somewhat to the east, has been considered classic; a massive polygonal wall, with a stone staircase of six steps, gave access to the levelled area of the shrine. An assumption has been put forth, that the fountain of K r i t e r i o n, which is known through literary sources, and which served as the area where the Argives held court and passed judgement, was located at this site. According to local tradition, king Danaos had passed judgement on Hypermestra, who had saved Lygeus, against his orders, at this very location, the "Kriterion". With regards to "the area where the Argives used to hold court", we have evidence that it was located at Prona, a hill to the south of the nymphaion, near the shrine of Aphrodite (see below). The goddesses Eumenides or Epitelides, patrons of childbirth, (both names are known through votive inscriptions of women about to bear a child), were honoured by the Argive women, at the sanctuary of the Nymphaion.

The t h e a t r e (number **8** on the plan, p. 96), had parts of its cavea and orchestra carved out of the natural rock, and, as a result, is in a fairly good state of preservation. The rows of benches which had been carved out of the natural rock, are supplemented by two wings of additional benches, to the right and left, and a number of intact rows of benches close to the orchestra. These additional benches were also made of rock. The cavea was given its final form during the 4th century B.C., when the first circular orchestra, of a 26-metre diameter, was constructed. It has been calculated that the theatre with 81 rows of benches, which were divided in three sections by two partitions, had a capacity of 20,000 spectators. During the roman era, the orchestra and the skene (stage) had been restored repeatedly, and given an entirely new form.

The imposing brick edifice of the t h e r m a i (roman baths) which belongs chronologically to the reign of the Antonines (close to the middle of the second century A.D.) have been preserved, in certain sections, to a height of 10 metres. The hot-air spaces (hypocausts), which had the sweating rooms built above them, are in a good state of preservation. In certain areas, in fact, parts of the mosaic floors are still intact.

The a g o r a of ancient Argos (number **10** on the plan, p. 96) was located east of the thermai, in an area which is inhabited in the present. Limited excavations have revealed arcades with colonnades, the foundations of houses, temples, and streets. Indications show that a central exposed area was surrounded on all four sides by long arcades. One of these, 83,5 metres long and 5,5 metres wide, has been revealed in its entirety. The columns of the façade, which faced the agora, were doric (the lower drums have been preserved in situ). The lower section of the marble frieze of a small circular edifice of the roman period, which in all probability was a fountain, bore columns of the corinthian order, along with the architrave, and the frieze. A large square edifice of the classical period, with sides 32,6 metres long, and columns on the inside, resembles the "Bouleuterion" (council hall) of Sikyon to the point that this, too, has been considered a bouleuterion, as well. The lower sections of four ionic colonnades, each consisting of 4 columns, are also in evidence. A small gymnasium, or wrestling area used to be part of the agora. The renowned gymnasium of Kylarabes, however, which bore the name of the mythical king, Kylarabes, was located outside the city walls, supposedly in the general area of the contemporary church of St. Constantine. Floor-mosaics of one of the late-roman edifices, which are located to the north of the main agora, those of another edifice which depict the twelve months of the year along with their symbols, as well as a mosaic with the representation of a dionysiac scene have been well preserved.

The O d e u m, a small theatre-like edifice, to the south of the large theatre, was cleared and exposed only recently. A number of the 18 semi-circular rows of benches, which are divided in two sections by a partition, have been carved, in this case as well, out of the natural rock. The remaining rows had been constructed with flat bricks, as was customary during the late roman period. Bricks had been used in the construction of the "skene" (stage), which had a second storey, or an elevated proscenium (a colonnade six to eleven feet deep and eight to thirteen feet high between the orchestra and the scene building, often terminated at either end with a parascenium), an assumption strengthened by the existence of the remains of a staircase near the right-side entrance to the stage. The orchestra is semi-circular, with a floor of imbedded marble, consisting of geometric motifs along the edges and sculptured scenes in the middle. This was true of the floors of the stage-entrances which carried vaulted roofs. The façade of the proscenium (facing the orchestra and the cavea) had been decorated with niches, which were fashionable in odeums of the late roman period.

At the beginning of the 4th century B.C., or even earlier, a theatre-like area had been set aside at the location of the odeum. This area had 35 s t r a i g h t r o w s o f b e n c h e s, carved out of the rock and divided in two sections by a partition. The demos of Argos used to assemble in this area during the pre-roman period (the area had been characterized as the "pnyx of the Argives"). An inscription from the neighbouring temple of Aphrodite gives the name Prona to the area of the shrine, as

75. The area of the agora of Argos which was located between the theatre (to the right) and the odeum (to the left), and which has been studied and excavated by the French School of Archaeology in Athens.

76. Larissa of Argos, as viewed from Deiras. To the left, the church of "Our Virgin of the Rock".

77. The shrine of Pythian Apollo near Deiras of Argos. The large altar which was carved in the rock is visible, along with the steps that were carved out of the same rock, and led to the upper terrace. To the right, the ruins of a large christian basilica.

78. Another view of the medieval fortifications of Larissa of Argos.

well as the Odeum, while an ancient source refers to Prona as the area where the Argives used to assemble in order to hold court and pass judgment. It is uncertain whether this theatre-like area, with the straight rows of benches could be identified with the Kriterion which has already been identified (without certainty, however) on the level area in front of the nymphaion at the foot of the hill of Larissa.

The shrine of Aphrodite, whose location was unknown until recently, was discovered and excavated a short distance (25 metres) to the south of the odeum (number **12** on the plan p. 96). The area of the shrine had been inhabited from the middle-helladic period (from the beginning of the second millennium B.C.), but the sanctuary itself, in the form of a simple temple, was no older than 630 or 620 B.C. Aside from the enclosure and the altar that had been constructed, it is possible that, a century later, a small temple had been built for the purpose of housing a "xoanon" (a crude and primitive image of a deity, carved in wood). The larger temple, however, whose stone foundations have been preserved (dimensions 13,4 × 6,2 metres) with two columns in antis at the "pronaos" (the porch in front of the naos or cella), is no older than the beginning of the peloponnesian war (430-420 B.C.). Votive inscriptions dedicated by women, to Aphrodite, have been discovered along with an inscribed pedestal, which was also located in the vicinity, and represented a priestess of the goddess. The site of the shrine of Pron is mentioned on the inscription of this pedestal.

The conical and precipitous hill of the Fort (Kastron), which is 289 metres high, used to be the main acropolis of ancient Argos, L a r i s s a. The ascent to the fortified top could be managed by a path which was not particularly steep. This path begins at the site of the odeum and reaches the southern entrance of the medieval fort. A few travelers make this ascent, nowadays, either on foot or by horse. Most of the visitors prefer the paved road which begins at Deiras, by-passes the north and west slopes of the hill, and reaches the same entrance of the medieval fort. The m e d i e v a l f o r t, which is in a rather good state of preservation (number **1** on the plan), consists of a roomy external fortified enclosure (approximately 200 metres, at the greatest length) and a smaller enclosure at the top (with an interior area 70 metres long). The smaller enclosure, which is surrounded by the larger one, used to

be the area prepared for a last stand (this being true of other forts, as well), in the event the besiegers had penetrated the outer defenses. The building of both forts shows many styles of construction, each side forming a straight line. Many sections, especially in the north and west sides, are superposed on the ancient greek wall which stands out and is easily identified by the large stones which have been used in the building without the benefit of mortar, while the medieval parts have been built with smaller stones and mortar. The polygonal style of construction of the ancient wall allows us to date it in the classical period. The construction of the medieval fort is supposed to have started in the 10th century, and was completed in the 13th during the frankish occupation of the area. Later on, the Venetians and the Turks, who held the neighbouring forts of Akronauplia and Palamidi from time to time, restored all of them. The ruins of a small christian church can be seen in the external enclosure. It has been constructed with many large blocks of stone, taken from ancient buildings, along with smaller common stones. According to an inscription mentioned in a report, in the Bulletin de Correspondence Hellenique, concerning the excavations of W. Vollgraff in 1928, this church had been restored by Manuel A' Komnenos in 1175. Vollgraff had excavated, in the area of the fort, in search of pre-christian structures. He discovered the porous foundations of two temples, which are known from literary sources to have been dedicated to Zeus Iarissaios, and Athena polias. According to Vollgraff, two statuettes, a clay and a bronze one, are pre-classical, along with an inscription which had been immured in the medieval

79. A small christian church, built inside the medieval acropolis of Argos with ancient architectural members.

80. Geometric "crater" from Argos; in the middle, a painted representation of two horses facing each other, and three women dancing, on the left.

81. Geometric "crater" (mixing bowl) from Argos of the 8th century B.C. The handles are perpendicular. Horizontal decorated bands are visible, the most significant one being the one above the cavity, a band which is divided, by perpendicular lines, into squares. The two squares that stand out have been decorated with two horses facing each other. The empty areas in both have been filled with birds.

fort, and refers to the sanctuary of "Athena polias". Potsherds, not only of the historical period (classic, archaic, geometric), but of the prehistoric (mycenaean and middle-helladic) periods, as well, have been found throughout the entire area of the fort. It is certain that the site had been inhabited during prehistoric times, when it was probably fortified; (that wall, whose parts have been considered cyclopean by Vollgraff, has been preserved on the south, east, and north slopes of the hill). Cisterns of water have been preserved in both enclosures of the medieval fort.

A precipitous drop of the rock, and a cave, which are located on the slope of Larissa above Argos at a considerable height above the houses of the city, purportedly had housed the ancient shrine of H e r a a k r a i a (number **6** on the plan). The church of "Panagia tou Vrachou" (Our Virgin of the Rock), known in the past as "katakekrymene" (one who is well hidden) is located on this site, and used to be part of a post-byzantine monastery. The site is accessible by a winding uphill road which begins at Deiras.

The second acropolis of Argos (80 metres high) was located at the top of the hill of prophet Elias (Elijah) (number **5** on the plan). This hill is a defile of the higher acropolis of Larissa, which in antiquity was named D e i r a s. We have no knowledge of the name given this fortified hill in the past. In the present one comes upon the church of prophet Elias which has been built on the very same hilltop. In later years, the name A s p i s was given to this area. It is evident, however, from literary sources, that the inaccessible site above the theatre was called Aspis, at one time along with the entire hill of Larissa.

An amphitheatrically-shaped site, which was suitable to the curve of the s t a d i u m, is formed at the western end of this defile before the hill begins to slope upwards towards the hill of prophet Elias. It has, therefore, been assumed by scholars that this area must have been the stadium of Argos, where the gymnastic contests of the festival of the Heraia used to take place in the late historical period (there is no suitable area for the contests near the shrine of the Heraeum, only a site suitable for games that did not require space). Even the games of the Nemeia (or the "winter Nemeia") used to take place in this very stadium during the era when the Argives had taken over the organization of these games, instead of the citizens of Kleonai.

Two important Argive temples have been excavated at Deiras: that of Apollo "deiradiotes", and that of Athena "oxyderkes" (clear-sighted). The road that led from the defile to the top of the hill used to pass by these two adjoining temples (number **3** on the plan, p. 97). The foundations and sections of the walls of a large christian basilica have been preserved on the site of these two shrines, as well as those of a smaller, older basilica, which had been replaced by the large one. In order to erect the large church with all its adjoining buildings, practically all the foundations of the ancient edifices were destroyed. The large rectangular altar of Apollo, which had been carved out of the natural rock, may be seen in a good state of preservation; it is 0,75 centimetres high, 14,32 metres long, and 3,21 metres wide. The altar rests on a foundation which is 16 metres long, and is carved out of the natural rock, along with the base of the altar. A staircase of 10 steps, whose width reaches 27 metres, had also been carved in the rock. This staircase is also in a good state of preservation, in spite of the fact that its southern section has been destroyed by the walls of the narthex (fore-court) of the christian church. Similar walls were also erected along the southern section of the altar, leaving the staircase and the altar intact, merely covering their south edges. These steps were used as benches by those who observed the sacrifices and other sacred events conducted on the large altar. They could also be used as a staircase which gave access to a higher level, on the east, where other sanctuaries were located. The temples of Apollo and Athena, as well as the oracle which was located on the same site, cannot be identified from the scant and inadequate ruins of the site. The foundations of two edifices, to the north of the altar, probably belong to stoas. A small section of the foundations of a circular structure (tholos) are in evidence to the east of the christian basilica. A large four-sided cistern, which supposedly belonged to a shrine on that site (according to one view, an Asclepieion), has been preserved to the north of this circular structure. It is certain that worship in the shrines of Deiras (not at the site of the presumed Asklepieion) was vigorous and strong, even during the archaic period. The large altar acquired its present form when the temples were restored in the fourth century. Inscriptions of the years close to 300 B.C. bear witness to the restoration of the temple of Apollo.

A p r e h i s t o r i c c e m e t e r y has been excavated in an area somewhat below the shrines of Deiras, to the right of the contemporary, as well as the ancient road, which led from the city to the gate of Deiras. These are mycenaean chamber tombs, and rectangular pit graves, which are not only mycenaean, but belong to the middle-helladic period, as well.

It is certain that during the middle-helladic period (approximately 2000 B.C.), an establishment had been built on the hill of Deiras, not only at the top, but also on its slopes. There were other middle-helladic setlements on the site of the contemporary city, at the foot of the hill of Larissa, especially in the area close to the theatre. Those of the late middle-helladic period are not the only ones represented among the finds that have been discovered so far. Following the second half of the late-helladic era, these finds become progressively more abundant, and habitation of the hill of Deiras is continuous. reaching the medieval period.

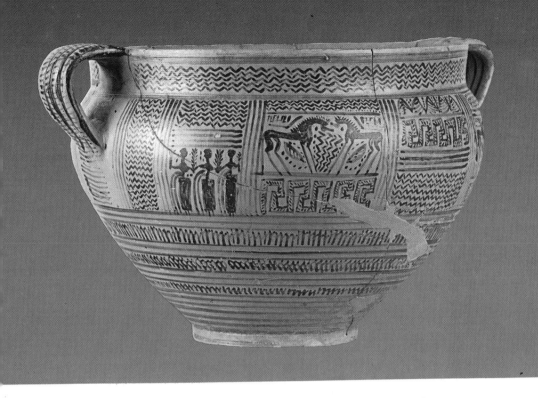

82. To the left, the brick ruins of the group of roman baths in Argos. To the right, the foundations of public edifices which are currently being excavated.

83. The theatre of Argos. The statuettes that are carved in the rock of the cavea of the orchestra, and of the skene are quite visible. To the right, the imposing ruins of the roman baths. The city of Argos in the background.

84. The ruins of the walls and building-foundations on the a-cropolis of Tiryns. **1.** The inclined ramp leading to the entrance. **2.** The entrance to the acropolis during the last building phase. **3.** The main gate which bears many similarities to the Lion gate of Mycenae. **4.** A small court-yard between the walls. **5** and **6.** Two gates which were not used concurrently. **7.** Roomy court-yard; a stoa on the east side with a colonnade facing the court-yard. **8.** Probable site of a staircase descending towards the eastern gallery and the six rooms located there. **9.** Large "propylon". **10.** Court-yard. **11.** Staircase descending to the south gallery, and the five small rectangular rooms located there. Before the construction of the gallery and the rooms, the stair-case used to lead to a small gate in the outer wall. **12.** Bulky tower of the south-west corner of the fortified enclosure. **13.** Small "propylon". **14, 15,** and **16.** Stoas on the west, south, and east side of the court-yard located before the megaron. **17.** Court-yard before the large megaron of Tiryns, and altar near the east column "in antis" of the propylon. **18, 19,** and **20.** Large megaron in Tiryns. **21.** Baths. **22.** Back court-yard. **23.** Small megaron. **24.** Court-yard of the small megaron. **25.** East side of the small megaron. **26.** Tower at the western branch of the wall. **27.** Staircase, in the interior of the sickle-shaped section of the wall, the one which leads to the tower. **28.** Small west gate of the wall. **29** and **30.** Small gates in the northern extension of the enclosure. **31.** Secret galleries descending to-wards the subterranean water-cisterns. **32** and **33.** Small build-ings, probably housing those in charge of the maintenance of the galleries and the water cisterns. **34.** Large structure, attached to the wall, which was probably used as a public storage warehouse. **35.** A house, shaped as a megaron, and located at the eastern foot of the hill. Farther to the east, the foundations of other houses.

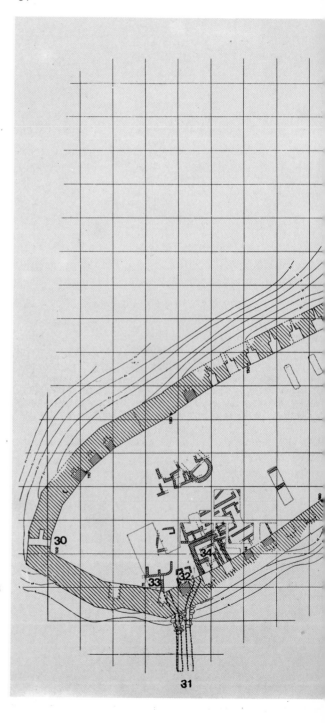

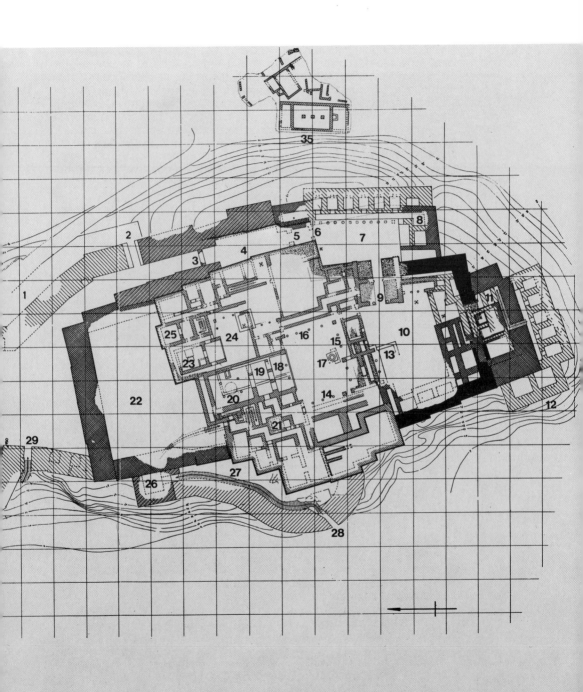

5. Tiryns

The fortified acropolis of Tiryns is located at a distance of seven kilometres south-east of Argos, to the right of the paved road and the railroad tracks that run between Argos and Nauplion. Built on a rocky hill, it is a mere 18 metres higher than the surrounding plain. During the prehistoric period, the south side of the hill, which happens to be its highest point, as well, was the first to be surrounded by a fortified wall. The north side, which is approximately 8 metres lower than the south, was fortified at the end of the mycenaean period and constituted a "lower acropolis". Houses have been excavated recently outside the acropolis, at the eastern foot of the hill. The area of the "lower acropolis" shows signs of habitation, not only after the building of the wall, but even earlier, at a period concurrent with that of the higher area of the hill. Houses were also discovered in the immediate vicinity, to the west which has always had an adequate supply of water.

The present walls and ruins of those buildings, which are extant in Tiryns, belong to a final stage or phase of construction in 1250-1200 B.C. Following a description of the shape and form of the acropolis, a summary of those conclusions that concern the earlier building phases will be presented.

A. The eastern access to the megaron

The entrance to the acropolis (number **2** on the plan, p. 111) was made accessible by an inclined ramp (number **1**), and not a staircase, thus facilitating the ascent of those animals that were kept in the "lower acropolis", near the houses of their owners, to the right of the entrance. Only a section of this inclined plain has been preserved, and has been given the shape of a ramp which, however, has neither the length, nor the width of the original ancient ramp. The original ramp began at that point of the wall, where the enclosure forms an obtuse angle (number **1**), and had a width of 4,7 metres, while its length was more than 45 metres. The entrance (number **2**) to the fort, originally, had a similar opening of 4,7 metres. Later on the opening was limited to 2,5 metres and has been preserved in that condition ever since. Upon passing through opening **2**, one headed to the left towards gate **3**, which had a great similarity with the lion gate of Mycenae, and, at the time that it was built, constituted the external gate of the fortification walls of Tiryns (the walls to the left and right of the gate were at least 8 metres high with a corridor of only 5 metres running between them). The stone threshold of this gate is still extant today, and has an approximate length of 4 metres, and a width of 1,5 metres, with stone pilasters, 3,2 metres high. The opening between the pilasters, which was somewhat less than 3 metres wide, used to be closed off with double doors (it might have been a wooden door with a lining of bronze). Its similarity to the lion gate permits one to assume that a similar relieving triangular stone slab must have been placed over the flat roof of the interior of the gate, as well. In Tiryns, this roof rested on the two sides of a wall which was 4,27 metres long, and had the same width as the corridor before the gate, which widens beyond this point.

The traces of two other gates (numbers **5** and **6**) are visible on the inside end of corridor **4**. It is improbable that both gates were in use simultaneously for any length of time. Court-yard **7** follows next, with a stoa of 12 columns at its eastern side. Underneath the stoa there is a gallery, which is approximately 29 metres long and 1,65 metres wide, and has the shape of a pointed corbelled arch throughout its entire length. This gallery gave access to a row of 6 rectangular rooms which have been assumed to have served as storehouses. The descent to the gallery was accomplished with the aid of a staircase which must have been located at point **8**.

The western side of court-yard **7** led to the large "propylon" **9** (the entrance

85. The acropolis of Tiryns (contemporary condition).

gate-building of an enclosure when there is one doorway only), which was a square construction, with sides approximately 13,5 metres long; the wall had a door in the middle, and stoas with two columns in front and back (the appearance of the façade which faces court-yard **10** is rather uncertain). The roomy court-yard **10** follows next, which must have served as an access to the southern gallery that was 22 metres long, and approximately 2,60 metres wide. In the gallery, five doors led to five small rectangular rooms. One could reach this gallery following staircase **11,** which was shaped in a right angle, and used to lead to a small gate of this fortified wall, at the time of the older fortification wall (before the gallery and the rooms had been constructed). Tower **12,** which is located at the southwest corner of the wall is contemporary to the gallery and the five rectangular areas.

B. The Interior Court and the Large Megaron

A smaller "propylon" (number **13**) used to lead from courtyard **10** to the interior court **17** (20,25 metres long, and 15,75 metres wide) with stoas (numbers **16, 15, 14**) at the east, south and west sides. The so-called "hall" of the megaron with two columns "in antis" is located at the north end. The traces of an altar, whose foundations have been considered prehistoric, but, which was in use even during the historical period, had been restored numerous times (in later years it was given a four-sided shape), and is located at the central axis of the megaron, near "propylon" **13.** All the columns of the court-yard stoas, and of the two halls of the megaron were made of wood, with stone bases. Most bases are in situ, due to the fact that they had been firmly imbedded rather deep in the floor.

The three areas of the megaron were arranged as follows: the outer "hall" (number **18** on the plan) was open towards the court and bore two columns in antis. The floor, which could be reached by two stone steps, had been paved with plaster, and embellished with decorative motifs inside squares. All along their lower parts,

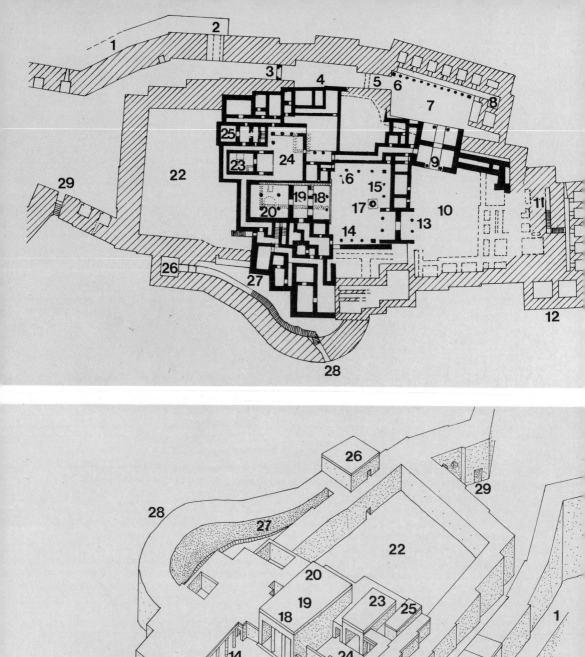

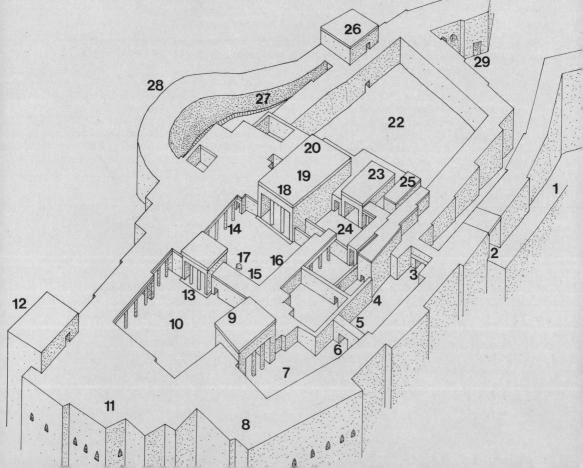

the walls carried a wide decorative band of alabaster slabs with "anthemia" (a pattern of alternating palmette and lotus motifs, often rising from nests of acanthus leaves and connected by scrolls) and rosettes, with round pieces of blue glass embedded between them (it has been assumed that the Odyssey refers to this "blue frieze" when describing the palace of Alkinoos, Book n,87). Frescoes had been painted above this band. This "hall" communicated with the next inner hall, the "prodomos" (corresponding to the porch in ordinary houses), (number **19** on the plan) through 3 doors. This hall had been decorated in a similar manner, along the walls and the floor. Finally, a door, in the middle of the north wall, gave access to the "prodomos", or the innermost hall, "the megaron" per se in other words, which had a hearth in the middle and a throne at the east wall (number **20** on the plan). This hall, with dimensions of 11,8 × 9,8 metres, had a floor with even richer decorations. The bases of the four columns, which supported the beams of a flat roof, have been preserved in situ around the circular hearth; an opening, which had been raised above the roof-level by small columns, had been constructed in the middle, and served as an outlet for the smoke rising from the hearth. This opening was covered by another roof, which prevented the rain from pouring inside the "hall".

C. The Cult of Hera and Athena in Tiryns

Following its destruction, it seems that the megaron of Tiryns was restored, and inhabited again until the sub-mycenaean period. During the early geometric period, however, an elongated structure was built on the same site, one which was approximately 21 metres long and 7 metres wide, and is believed to have been a temple dedicated to Hera; one wall rests on the east wall of the megaron; the west wall was built on new foundations in the middle of the megaron. The cult of Hera has been ascertained through tradition, as well, according to which the first argolid shrine of the goddess had been established in Tiryns by Peirasos, the son of Argos, and grandson of Zeus. When the Argives destroyed Tiryns after the persian wars, they took the old cult statue of Hera from the shrine (this small wooden image depicted the goddess in a sitting position) and carried it to their own Heraeum (see p. 19 above). It is also certain that, aside from Hera, Athena and Zeus were also worshipped in Tiryns during the early archaic period; inscriptions carved on the rocks in the southern gallery (number **31** on plan, p. 110) refer to the gods "ΔίϜα κ' 'Αθαναίαν" — Zeus and Athena. The cult of Athena, especially, is certain, judging from the 4th century head of a clay statuette of the goddess, as well as votive inscriptions, one of them carved on a fragment of a clay "krater" (a large vessel or bowl originally used for mixing wine with water). An "old-fashioned" doric capital, which belonged to an early temple, was discovered in Tiryns, along with fragments of an archaic gutter, lined with clay which bore carved decorations.

D. Building Ruins in the Vicinity of the Great Megaron

The foundations of many walls are to be found to the west of the mycenaean megaron. Some of these belong to houses, others to staircases, and others still to sky-lights and narrow passages. The staircases had been constructed out of wood,

86 and 87. Ground plan (above) and reconstruction (below) of the main edifices on the acropolis of Tiryns. Each structure bears the same number in both plans, and in the overall plan 84. 1. Inclined ramp to the entrance. 2. Exterior opening to the gate. 3. The gate. 4. Small court-yard. 5. Smaller gate. 6. Gate not used concurrently with 5. 7. Larger court-yard. 8. Stone staircase. 9. Exterior "propylon". 10. External court-yard. 11. Staircase built inside the thickness of the wall. 12. Tower. 13. "Propylon" to the megaron. 14, 15, and 16. Stoas of the interior court-yard. 17. Altar. 18, 19, and 20. Megaron. 22. Open area in the back of the megaron. 23. Small megaron. 24. Court-yard of small megaron. 25. Third, smaller megaron. 26. Tower. 27. Stone staircases in the interior of the wall. 28. Western small gate 29. Small gate leading to the west.

or stone, and led from one storey to the next; those scholars which dispute the existence of a second storey in these apartments, believe that the staircases merely led to the level roofs (terraces) of the various buildings. The narrow area **19** was used as a bathroom; its floor consists of one large block of stone which had a smooth upper surface with a groove carved into it for the draining of water. The western wall of the "prodomos" (porch) of the large megaron (number **19**) had a door which led to the apartments to the west. Another staircase (number **22**) also led from the back court of the palace, to these very same apartments.

A narrow passage, which was shaped in a right angle, and was located behind the large megaron, led to the eastern apartments which were also of great importance. A small megaron (number **23**) was located on that site and seems to have been built before the large one. The small megaron had a courtyard in front which was surrounded by stoas (number **24**). Further to the east, one comes upon the traces (number **25**) of an even smaller structure of the megaron type.

E. The Western Branch of the Fortification Wall

Tower **26,** of the western fortification wall, secured, at an early period the northwest corner of the enclosure, and later on staircase **27** and the small gate **28**. The staircase is well protected by the heavy sickle-shaped section of the wall. The small gate **28** was located at its lower section and was the kind of gate that could not be forced even in the event that the door had been left unlocked. It was impossible for a group of people to pass through it simultaneously, and the one or two persons who might get past could easily be exterminated by the defenders on the wall. In the event one reached the staircase, it was difficult to reach tower **26**, through which one had to pass before entering the acropolis. Even if one were able to reach the top of the staircase, one could not enter the tower because the space between that and the staircase was empty, covered by a wooden bridge (when this was required), which could be withdrawn, or even left in position, only to give way when stepped upon, in which case any invader would fall quite suddenly and unexpectedly from a height of 7 metres.

F. The Extension of the Fortification Wall to the North

The north section of the acropolis, which is also the lowest, had been inhabited in the early helladic era, but had been left unfortified for a period of 1000 years. When the external dangers for all mycenaean acropoleis increased in the years 1250-1200 B.C., the northern section was fortified, thus doubling the enclosed defensible area. The thickness of the new wall reached 8 metres. Many large, undressed blocks of stone, with uneven courses were used in its construction. The building began with the east side wall at gate **3,** which until then had served as the external gate of the enclosed area, and a new entrance was shaped on the outside (opening **2**). The western extension ended at the transverse section of the wall of the upper acropolis (that close to tower **26**). The eastern one (number **2**) was the main entrance to the lower acropolis. This was accessible through a small gate at the west side, which could be approached by a staircase (number **29** plan on p. 110), and by another one on the north side (number **30**). The underground cisterns of water, which were actually located outside the wall (number **31**), were made accessible, from the inside of the new wall, through the galleries; this secured an adequate supply of water in the event of a siege. An assumption has been made that, public servants, for whom the city had built special quarters at the gallery-entrances (numbers **32** and **33**), had been in charge of the maintenance of both the galleries and the underground cisterns. A large structure (number **34**), which might have

88. The corridor between the walls, which led to the apartments of the megaron in Tiryns.

been used as a public warehouse (as the case was with public buildings), was attached to one of the fortification walls.

The fortified area of the lower acropolis shows evidence of continuous habitation even in the historical period. Traces of later buildings were unearthed along with prehistoric ruins.

G. Ruins Outside the Acropolis

A large megaron, with three separate sections along its length, has been excavated at the east foot of the hill, a short distance from the eastern gallery. Of the three sections, the main one (11 × 7 metres) was located in the middle and had three interior roof-supports (their stone bases have been preserved along a straight line). A hearth had been built between two of these roof-supports. The building had been in use around 1200 B.C. Another house, with a rectangular main room (7,4 × 4,2 metres), was discovered further to the east. It had a four-sided hearth in the middle, and two smaller areas on the outside of its north wall. Other sections, which were probably used as warehouses, had been built outside the south wall. Chronologically, the second house is older than the former two (the last one has been dated in 1430 B.C., or thereabouts), and was excavated on the same site, at a deeper level.

Some ruins of houses, which were chronologically older (middle-helladic), have been excavated to the southeast of the acropolis, and others have been discovered to the west, next to the railway track, and paved main road.

A tholos tomb, with a diameter of 8,5 metres, and a "dromos" 13 metres long and 3 metres wide has been known to exist for a long time, at the foothill of prophet Elias, and a distance of approximately one kilometre east of the acropolis. The walls of the "dromos" have been lined with a wall of small irregular undressed stones. Chronologically, the tholos belongs to the end of the mycenaean period.

H. Phases in the Building Activity of Tiryns

Neolithic potsherds and one neolithic statuette, which were found in Tiryns, allow us to deduce that the hill had been inhabited even during neolithic times. On the other hand, however, there is no evidence, or trace of buildings older than the second half of the middle-helladic period. A circular structure is one that has been studied the most. It had a diameter of approximately 28 metres, a circumference of approximately 88 metres, and had been built shortly before 2000 B.C. Small stones and unbaked clay bricks had been used as building material. Since this building is located under the large megaron, only that part which was outside the east wall of the megaron (in the court-yard of the small megaron) has been excavated. Shafts were driven near the hearth and the court-yard of the large megaron, thus

89. Inclined ramp leading to the acropolis of Tiryns.

substantiating the circular shape and the building technique used in this large middle-helladic structure. It is not known, however, whether it had a court-yard in the middle and rooms along its circumference, or whether it was a circular fort with a roofed area in the middle which was used for habitation.

It has been assumed that the first mycenaean acropolis had taken its final form around 1400 B.C. Its nucleus was located on the site of the large megaron and courtyards **17** and **10,** at a much lower stratus. A fortified enclosure with one gate only, was located at the site of what later on was to become "propylon" **9.** This gate had a narrow entrance with bulky towers to the right and left. To the north, it is probable that this enclosure included courtyard **22,** as well.

The acropolis was extended around 1300 B.C. The external gate (that on the site of "propylon" **9**) continued in use, while another gate was built on the outside, with two openings (**5** and **6**), and wooden doors between strong towers (it would seem that one of these doors was destroyed by a fire at an early date). A bulky bastion was built to the south, with a small entrance in the middle, which was made accessible by staircase **11** that was shaped in a right angle (the southern gallery and the five rectangular rooms had not been built as yet). The so-called small megaron (number **23**) had been in use at that very same time. There is no evidence of an early structure on the site of the large megaron. During this period (a little before 1250 B.C.) a stronger fortified external gate was built between the two tall branches of the wall, as was the case with the lion gate of Mycenae; the former bearing many similar

90. Exterior view of the walls of Tiryns (west side).

91

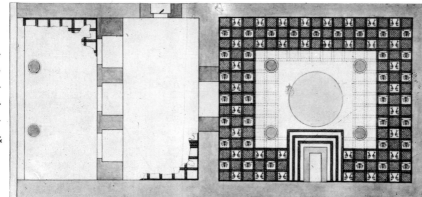

92 93

91. The court-yard and the megaron of Tiryns, seen from the internal "propylon" (no. **13** on pl. 86-87).

92. Ground plan of the megaron in Tiryns, with a decorated floor in all three rooms. The hearth was located in the innermost room, in the centre of four columns, and the throne had been placed in the middle of one of the side-walls.

93. The court-yard and megaron in Tiryns; in the present condition.

94. The stone staircase in the interior of the sickle-shaped branch of the wall (the west side of the fortified enclosure of Tiryns).

94

95

95. The ''galleries'' of Tiryns, built inside the thickness of the fortification wall, had been constructed with uncemented stone blocks.

96. Chronologically, the galleries belong to the last building phase of the acropolis. The stone-blocks inclining slightly towards the centre form a corbelled pointed arch.

97. Exterior view of the sickle-shaped section of the west wall of the acropolis. The small entrance leading to the stone staircase of picture 94 is visible in the middle.

98. Bronze helmet from Tiryns; of the sub-mycenaean, or early geometric period.

substantial characteristics of the latter (number **3**). It has been assumed, again, that the older gate **5** was still in use. Tower **26** was built during this period for the purpose of providing the western wall with a stronger defense, and offering protection to the small gate that was already located there.

Finally, the acropolis acquired its present fortifications in 1230 B.C.; the wall-enclosure was extended to the north and included the so-called lower acropolis, two sloped galleries were built, and led downward towards the water cisterns, the sickle-shaped section of the wall **26-28** was built, along with staircase **27** on the inside. The east gallery (number **8**) with the six square windows, and the south one with the 5 rooms were constructed along with the bulky tower **12** in the southwestern corner of the acropolis. Following the northern extension of the wall outwardly, opening **2** was used as an entrance gate, and could be reached by an inclined plain. In the interior, "propyla" **9** and **13**, and the large megaron **18, 19, 20** were constructed, while the older one, **23**, was still in use.

It is characteristic of this last phase of building activity that larger blocks of stone were used for the fortification walls than had been used in the past, and that the courses were not set in a straight line. In order to cover narrow areas, or passages, the workmen used the pointed corbelled arch which was created by courses of blocks of stone that converged towards the top.

After these mycenaean buildings had been destroyed, the acropolis and the city of Tiryns were still being inhabited, as far as can be deduced from the evidence of the ruins, not only of the geometric and archaic periods, but also of later periods in history, such as the byzantine, until the years of the Turkish occupation of the land. When excavations began, a small church was still standing on the hill (its site was the southern side of courtyard **10**, on top of the mycenaean foundations).

6. The Asklepieion of Epidaurus

The most convenient road to the Asklepieion of Epidaurus is the paved road from Nauplion-Ligourio, whose one branch, 5 kilometres long, reaches the sanctuary. The total distance from Nauplion is 28 kilometres.

The older myths concerning the origin of Asklepios connect him with Thessaly, or Messenia, and not with Epidaurus. Local tradition alone presents his mother Koronis — impregnated by Apollon — as a visitor to Epidaurus, along with her father Phlegyas, at which time she gave birth to Asklepios. Contrary to the myth, the cult of Asklepios has deep roots in the sanctuary of Epidaurus. All the other Asklepieia of Greece and Asia Minor are presumed dependent on the sanctuary of Epidaurus, where Asklepios was worshipped as a god (at a much later date, however).

The cult of epidaurian Asklepios is one of the most recent in Greece. Its expansion was rapid during the hellenistic and roman periods. Many local cults of healing gods or heroes were replaced by the cult of Asklepios.

Originally, god Maleatas, who, already during the pre-classical period, had been identified with Apollon, because the latter was a healing god, used to be worshipped at the site of the epidaurian Asklepieion. The shrine of Apollon Maleatas continued its separate existence during the centuries of the great prosperity of the Asklepieion. It was located at the top of mount Kynortion which rose over the theatre. It is apparent from the name, that the old god Maleatas had originally come from Maleatis of northern Parnon (Parnon was named Maleas throughout its entire length, from Kynouria to the cape which bears this name).

Before the 4th century B.C., there was no monumental edifice in evidence at the foot of Kynortion, where the sanctuary of Asklepios is located today. The Epidaurians had built a second shrine to Apollon in the city itself, by the seashore; a shrine which remained unchanged and did not alter in any way throughout antiquity. On the contrary, the inland sanctuary, which had ignored or pushed aside the worship of Maleatas, had already begun to acquire a panhellenic fame from the 5th century onward. It was one among the most famous and wealthiest sanctuaries during the 4th century and, before the end of the century, had been embellished with its main edifices, the temple of Asklepios, the tholos, the theatre and a few smaller marble temples (of Artemis, Aphrodite, and Themis). Following the introduction of games of prowess during the festival of Asklepios, the gymnasium, the wrestling area, the stadium, and most of the stoas and bathing facilities were added, and later on were increased in number during the imperial roman period, when the sanctuary underwent a new period of prosperity.

Contrary to the plans of other panhellenic sanctuaries, the Asklepieion was not restricted within an easily defined area, but expanded over an area of hundreds of metres, in such a way that one looks in vain for some pre-arranged ground plan according to which the religious and various other edifices and buildings had been constructed (one needs to walk the distance of one kilometre from the monumental "propylon", which constitutes the northern boundary of the sanctuary, to the central cluster of edifices with the temple and the tholos, to the stadium, the gymnasium, and the large guest-house, before one can reach the theatre. The same distance is required going uphill, in order to reach the shrine of Maleatas, having on the way, walked past the secluded marble temple which is located half-way between the two shrines).

A. The Stadium and the Theatre

Upon completion of the long-term excavations of the Asklepieion, a new access to the various edifices was constructed, one which is completely different from the ancient. The ancient Epidaurians wanted the entrance from the north, at the spot

99. The countryside around the Asklepieion of Epidaurus. The theatre is located on the left, and the shrine on the foregrounds to the right.

100. The Sanctuary of Asklepios in Epidaurus. **1.** The Stadium. **2.** The theatre. **3.** The guest-house, or "katagogeion". **4.** Pre-roman baths. **5.** Gymnasium. An Odeum was built inside its area. **6.** "Palaistra", or wrestling area, with the stoa of Kotys on the north side (Kavadias). **7.** Temple of Artemis. **8.** Temple of Asklepios. **9.** The tholos. **10.** "Abaton" or "Enkoimeterion", (sleeping areas for the ill). **11.** Roman baths. **12.** Large Stoa **13.** Imposing "propylaea" leading to the sanctuary. **14.** Small temple similar to that of Artemis; perhaps of Themis. (Plan by 'The Doxiades' Athens centre of Ekistics).

101

102

101. Contemporary view of the stadium, in the Asclepieion of Epidaurus.

102. The foundations of the "katagogeion" (place of rest or lodging) which have been excavated at the shrine of Asklepios.

103. Remains of the Gymnasium at the Asklepieion of Epidaurus.

104. The Odeum which was constructed during the roman period inside the level area of the gymnasium.

where the road from the city of Epidaurus reached the sanctuary, so they built a monumental "propylon" to the shrine on that site. From the "propylon", whose foundations are still in evidence today, one followed the "sacred way", which was approximately 200 metres long, to the temple of Asklepios and the tholos, leaving stoas, baths, and various other smaller buildings, connected with the shrine, to the left and the right of the way.

The contemporary road that reaches the theatre passes to the left of the s t a d i u m first (number **1** on the plan, p. 129). This occupies a natural depression of the ground near the temple and the tholos, and is a structure of the late classical period. This natural depression had been dug out along its entire length and width, while straight rows of stone benches were built along its north and south sides (but not along their entire length, however). The track was levelled, at approximately 23 metres of width and 181,10 metres of length from the starting point to the finish. It had a straight sphendone, not a curved one, as did other stadia. The conclusion is, therefore, reached that the track that was used for racing at the Asklepieion was more than 11 metres shorter than that of the olympic (where the length was 192,27 metres) and close to 4 metres shorter than that of the panathenaic stadium (its length was 184,96 metres).

The t h e a t r e of the Asklepieion (number **2** on the plan p. 129) (which has been generally considered the work of Polykleitos the Younger, who lived in the 4th century), is not considered any older than 300 B.C., if one takes into consideration the advanced original construction of the skene, and the "proskenium" (a colonnade between the orchestra and the skene building, often terminating at either end with a paraskenium), which was 3,5 metres higher than the orchestra. The latter formed a full circle, with a diameter of 20 metres, not only at the time of its construction, but even later after the various extensions and restorations that followed. In its original form, the cavea consisted of the lower rows of benches, with 12 tiers only. In order to obtain better acoustics, only 8 rows of benches of the 8 central tiers had been designed in such a way that their radii extended to the centre of the orchestra. The two tiers, to the right and the left, have a centre closer to the skene and their curves are segments of larger circumferences. The impression that the viewer gets, however, is that all the rows are segments of concentric circles. Shortly before the roman period, during a later restoration of the theatre, a "diazoma" (a horizontal passage which separated the several ranges of seats in a theatre or stadium) was formed, and the cavea was extended upward, with new rows of benches; 22 new tiers altogether, increased the number of seats of the theatre from 6,200 to 12,300. Twenty-one rows of benches were formed above the "diazoma", and were added to the 34 original ones of the lower section. One could reach the "diazoma" without going through the orchestra and the staircases between the tiers, but by using one of the two inclined ramps to the right and left of the entrance.

B. Buildings between the Theatre and the Temple

The museum of the sanctuary has been built a short distance from, and to the northwest of the theatre. In the same general northwest direction, beyond a small stream of water, and before the group of buildings which surround the temple of Asklepios, the foundations of a large, square, isolated building were excavated. Each side of the building was 76 metres long. It is certain that this structure (no **3**), which had stone foundations, with brick walls above them was used as a "katagogeion" — g u e s t   h o u s e — with numerous rooms which accommodated those visitors who wished to stay at the shrine during the festival of Epidaurus. It is believed to have had 2 storeys and a total number of 150 rooms. The large outer area had been divided into four equal smaller squares by a wall which started in the

105. Representation of the central buildings of the shrine of Asklepios: (the "tholos" to the left, the "enkoimeterion", or adytum (the inner or most holy room of a temple) in the background, the temple of Asklepios in the centre; (plan by A. Defrasse).

middle of the west side, and then another one which reached from the middle of the north side to the middle of the south side. Each of the four smaller square areas had a peristyle court in the centre. Each square had a total of 18 rooms around the courtyard. All the rooms had doors facing the court, and no communicating doors between them.

A rectangular pre-roman edifice (number **4** on the plan), with dimensions of approx. 35 × 25 metres, is located to the west of this large guest-house. This building used to be a b a t h connected to a large rectangular structure to the north — with dimensions of 75,6 × 69,5 metres — which used to be a g y m n a s i u m (number **5**). The gymnasium had a large interior peristyle court, with some small, and other large covered areas along its length, on all four sides. The so-called gymnasia, especially those in cities, but those in large sanctuaries, as well, were not used for gymnastics alone, but also as centres of numerous other cultural activities, which used to be attended, not only by the young men exercised there, but by all those citizens who were interested in them, as well (visiting philosophers used to give lectures, poetry was recited, various announcements were made, and debates took place). An imposing "propylon", which has been excavated near the northwest corner of the building, gave access to the courtyard of this gymnasium. The "propylon" had six doric columns on its façade and four columns on each of its sides (the east and west sides).

This large structure ceased to be used as a gymnasium, in the imperial roman times because the needs it fulfilled were taken over by more modern buildings. An o d e u m was built in its roomy interior court for the performance of musical programs, as well as lectures and recitals which used to be organized on the occasion of the festival of Asklepios. It had eleven or twelve curved rows of benches, constructed with bricks, according to the fashion of the late roman era (the lower benches are in situ, as well as sections of the skene which had also been built with bricks).

The next structure to the north (approximately 34 × 29,5 metres) had an open area in the centre, with stoas on the four sides and rooms on all its sides except the north, where a wider stoa, with a colonnade in the centre, used to be located. This entire structure has been considered a "palaestra" (wrestling area, number **6** on the plan). The stoa of Kotys, which is known through literary sources, is usually

106. The "cavea" of the theatre, at the Asklepieion of Epidaurus, as this has been restored. Bottom right: the foundations of "scene" construction. (The "orchestra" was a full circle until the end of antiquity).

identified with the roomy stoa of the north side. Lately, however, it has been assumed, that the stoa of Kotys could have been a larger one among the group of buildings which closed off, to the north, the central area of the sanctuary (number **12** in the plan).

A small "prostyle" temple follows next, with dimensions of 13,3 × 9,4 metres, and 6 doric columns in its façade. Through literary sources, it had been identified from the start, as the temple of Artemis (number **7** on the plan), which was located on the site of the main shrine. It consisted only of a "pronaos" (porch) and a cella. Colonnades of corinthian columns decorated the walls of the cella, close to the north, west, and south walls, without forming aisles, however.

C. The Temple and the Tholos

The construction of the temple of Asklepios, (no **8**) which was the creation of the architect, Theodotus, began at about 380 B.C. The "krepidoma" (the stepped platform of a greek temple) was 24,5 × 13,22 metres, and the "pteron" (the wing or flank colonnade of a temple) had 6 doric columns along the narrow ends, and eleven columns along the flanks. Access was attained by an inclined ramp, set in the centre of the east side. The temple had a "distyle pronaos" (a porch in front of the naos or cella) in antis, and a cella whose north and south walls had a colonnade of seven columns each; these were semi-detached columns, their function being mainly decorative, as they had been placed against the walls. The façade of the west wall was decorated with a similar colonnade of four columns. The cella contained a larger-than-life gold-and-ivory statue of Asklepios. It showed the god seated on a throne, with one hand resting on the head of a snake, and the other resting on a tall staff. A dog had been placed by the feet of the god. The statue was the creation of the scupltor Thrasymedes of Paros, a contemporary of the Athenian Praxiteles. Timotheos, a sculptor, of the 4th century, as well, was the creator of the pedimental sculptures. The triangular spaces of the pediments, the "tympana", were 10,7 metres long and 1,4 metres high at the apex of the pediment. The compositions of these pediments were the fall of Troy on the east front, and the battle of the Greeks and Amazons on the west. Ruins of the large altar of Asklepios are in evidence south of the temple (near the southeast corner).

The foundations of the tholos (number **9** on the plan) are in evidence to the

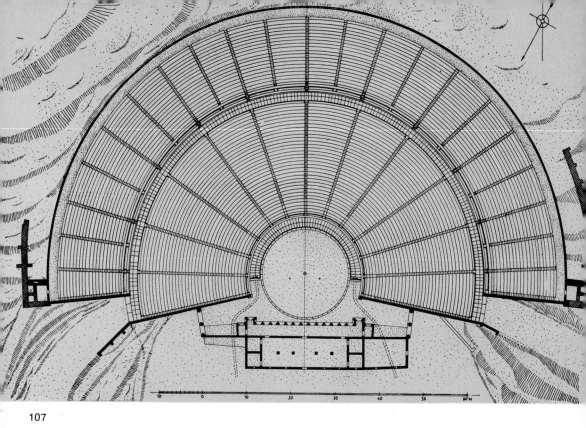

107. Floor plan of the theatre of Asklepios, during the hellenistic and roman period. The section of the cavea above the "diazoma" does not belong to the original plan, but constitutes a subsequent addition.

west of the temple. This was a circular structure of an external diameter of 21,8 metres. The "pteron" rose from a circular "stylobate" (the upper step of a temple, which formed a platform for the columns) with three steps. It had 26 doric columns, approximately 7 metres tall, which supported the circular architrave, and above that the circular frieze of triglyphs and metopes. A marble "anthemion" (floral piece of sculpture), an "acroterion" (figure or ornament at the apex of the roof, or the lower angles or apex of a pediment) rose to a height of 12 metres, at the top of the circular roof. The tholos followed the general plan of a "peripteros" (a temple whose cella is surrounded by a peristyle) temple, in that the wall of the cella, which was circular, had been built on the inside of the columns. It has been deduced that the dressed interior surface of the cella had been decorated with the composition of the Sikyonian painter Pausias. A second colonnade of 14 corinthian columns, 6,75 metres high, had been built inside the wall of the cella (corinthian capitals and sections of the entablature may be seen on that section of the tholos that has been restored in the museum of the Asklepieion). The entire floor of the tholos had been paved; the central area with romboidal alternating pieces of black and white marble. A round white slab of stone had been placed in the centre of the floor, and could be raised, allowing one a view of the area under the floor of the tholos. This underground area under the white stone, was circular, as well, and had a diameter of approximately 8 metres. In the past, it had been assumed that the valuable offerings to the temple were placed for safe-keeping in this area. Recently, however, scholars tend to agree that this underground area was used as a cult ritual pit, where offerings were made to Asklepios who was worshipped as a hero in the tholos, while he was honoured as a god in the temple. When the worship of Asklepios, as a hero, ceased, the sacred rituals, in the underground area of the tholos, ceased, as well. Three circular concentric stone walls, which had been built under its floor, are the only extant parts of the tholos today. The inner-most of these walls served as the

108. *The theatre, as viewed within the surrounding landscape.*

sub-structure upon which the inner-most corinthian colonnade rested; the wall in-between supported the circular wall of the cella, and the exterior one, which was thicker than the others, was the support of the circular stylobate and the pteron with the 26 external doric columns.

D. Other Building Ruins

The foundations of two adjoining stoas, of a total length of 71 metres, and a width of 9,5 metres, were excavated at a site to the north of the temple and the tholos. It had been assumed that these were used as "enkoimeteria" (sleeping areas) for the sick. Of those who were sick, some were cured after this sleep, the kind of treatment to be followed was revealed to others, while others used to leave having experienced no dream, a fact which was interpreted as an ill omen concerning the course of the illness. The attendants of the god, who had undertaken the care of a sick person, directed the kind of medication, and general treatment one ought to follow, were helped, on the most part, by the long-term experience they had acquired while serving at the sanctuary after a great number of years. One means of healing was cleanliness and bathing in the "thermai" (warm baths) of the Asklepieion. The section of the "enkoimeterion" which is located across the temple is considered the oldest (4th century B.C.). The one adjoining to the west (across from the tholos) was built the following century, and had two storeys because the ground is lower in that area; the remains of a staircase are in evidence on the exterior façade of the stoa. Both sections of the stoa had one colonnade each at the façade, and another one along the centre.

It has been deduced that another large four-sided structure (number **10** on the plan), which used to be located east of the temple and the altar of Apollon (immediately to the north of the temple of Artemis), had also been used as an "enkoimeterion" prior to the stoas described above. This building has also been taken for "a cluster of sacred buildings", or as the housing-quarters of the priests of the shrine.

A second elegant small hexastyle temple, which bears a great resemblance to the one (temple of Artemis on p. 135) mentioned above, was excavated on the left side of the road to the "propylaea" (number **14** on the plan). Its foundations have the dimensions of 13,56 × 7,42m. This small temple had a cella lined, on the inside, with corinthian colonnades along the north, south, and west walls. It is not certain, however, whether the façade was formed by a "prostasis" (porch), or simply by two ionic columns, in antis.

A third identical small temple was excavated outside the area of the main Asklepieion, uphill, on the way to the temple of Maleatas The façade had a colonnade of four (or six) ionic columns; the outside of the north and south walls of the cella had five ionic semi-columns, four semi-columns on the west wall, in a way that, along with the four columns of the façade, one was left with the impression of a peristyle temple. Twelve corinthian columns, engaged to the surface of the north, west, and south walls, had been placed inside the cella. Of these three temples, the temple of Artemis has been identified with certainty (number **7** on the plan). The other two belonged to Themis and Aphrodite.

The large propylaea of the shrine (number **13** on the plan), with a foundation of 20,27 × 14,39 metres, were a monumental structure on the "sacred way" which led to the temple of Asklepios. It had two façades, with six ionic columns each, one towards the outer, and the other towards the inner side of the shrine. The ascent to the upper part of the "krepidoma" was accomplished with inclined ramps which had been built at the centre of each façade. On the inside of the "propylon", a corinthian colonnade of five columns had been erected on each side, in front of the walls that closed the east and west sides. Four columns had been erected along each of the north and south sides, forming two sides that were tetrastyle in antis.

At the shrine of Apollon Maleatas, former excavations had revealed the temple of the god which was actually a small cella. In the immediate vicinity, to the northeast of the temple, a thick stone terrace wall, 45 metres long, has been excavated. Its southern façade created a stoa open to the central area of the sanctuary. To the south, this area was closed off with a fountain, and a cistern of the roman period, as well as a group of buildings which have been assumed to have been those known through inscriptions as "ἐπὶ Κυνὸς σκανάματα" (probably the housing quarters of the attendants of the god, and other secondary edifices on the sacred area). Recent excavations seem to reveal older remains than those of the Asklepieion. The traces of an altar of Maleatas, which belonged with certainty to the early archaic period, have been excavated near the northeast corner of the small temple.

109. Cross-section and reproduction of the interior of the "tholos". The exterior colonnade of the circular "pteron" belongs to the doric order. The circular wall of the structure can be seen next, followed, on the inside, by the circular corinthian colonnade. The engraved sculptured decoration of the interior surface of the wall can be seen on the upper part of the wall.

110. The foundations of the "tholos" in their present condition.

111. The foundations of the temple of Asklepios, bearing an inclined ramp at the entrance (east side).

112. Ground plan of the temple of Asklepios (G. Roux).

113. A reproduction of the eastern flank of the temple of Asklepios. It is evident, from the sculptured fragments that have been found on the site, that one of the pedimental compositions represented an amazonomachie. Fragments of the equestrian female figures which were used as "akroteria" have also been found here.

1

COUPE RESTAURÉE DE LA THOLOS

112

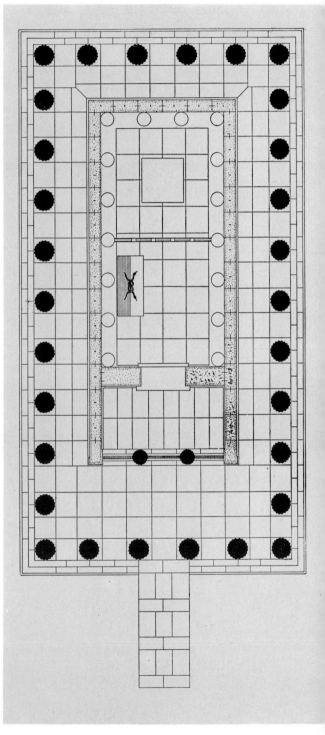

4. Headless female
statue, purportedly
representing the goddess
Hygieia.

5. The trunk of another
female statue at the
museum of the Asklepieion.
The "gorgon" head seems
to indicate that it belongs to
the goddess Athena.

116. One of the numerous statues of Asklepios, "the beardless", as the god was often depicted in various shrines of Greece during the period of late antiquity.

117. An equestrian female figure which served as an "acroterion" (the figure or ornament at the lower angles or apex of a pediment) of the temple of Asklepios (the work of the sculptor Timotheos).

118. Sections of the sculptured decoration of the ceiling coffers of the tholos at the shrine of Asklepios.

119. The corinthian capital at the Asklepieion, that which is considered the prototype of all hellenistic capitals of this type.

118